Growing together

A practice guide to promoting social inclusion through gardening and horticulture

Joe Sempik, Jo Aldridge and Saul Becker

Supported by

First published in Great Britain in May 2005 by

The Policy Press
University of Bristol
Fourth Floor, Beacon House
Queen's Road
Bristol BS8 1QU
UK

Tel no +44 (0)117 331 4054
Fax no +44 (0)117 331 4093
E-mail tpp-info@bristol.ac.uk
www.policypress.co.uk

© Loughborough University, in association with Thrive 2005

Reprinted 2008
Transferred to Digital Print 2011

ISBN 978-1-86134-726-8

Joe Sempik (BSc, MSc, PhD) is a Research Fellow in the Centre for Child and Family Research, Loughborough University. **Jo Aldridge** (BA, PhD) is a Research Fellow in the Department of Social Sciences, Loughborough University. **Saul Becker** (BA, MA, CQSW, PhD) is Professor of Social Care and Health at the University of Birmingham.

All photographs produced in this guide were taken by Joe Sempik and Jo Aldridge, unless otherwise stated.

Cover design by Qube Design Associates, Bristol
Printed and bound by CPI Group (UK) Ltd, Croydon, CR0 4YY

Contents

Foreword

The calming and restorative powers of plants and of nature are increasingly valued as a means of helping people escape from the pressure and competition of our technology-driven world, where it is so easy to forget that all living things are connected.

This guide is being published at a time when throughout the world some wonderful projects are making use of the social and therapeutic power of horticulture to enhance people's lives through regaining their connection with the earth.

When the Sheltered Work Opportunities Project started out 15 years ago, there was no such guide available – indeed there were very few other independent charity-based horticultural projects when we opened Cherry Tree Nursery in 1990.

We provide meaningful work rehabilitation in a shrub nursery for adults with severe and enduring mental illness. We are committed to offering a supportive family environment where each person feels needed, valued, important and included, and can regain their place in society and in the local community. We provide routine, structure and a wide range of work skills. We strive to counter the stigma and discrimination so often experienced by people with mental illness, and to offer a space where people can learn to laugh again and to support and care for each other while sharing in the joy of growing plants.

We started with only four clients, a short-term lease of two acres of land, one member of staff and a £1,000 interest-free loan from a supporter. Now, 15 years later, we have over a hundred clients, a lease of four-and-a-half acres of land and six staff. We have gained recognition in many ways including the Queen's Golden Jubilee Award in 2003, and, in November 2004, the Lilly Reintegration Award Recognising Outstanding Achievement in Mental Health.

We believe these achievements reinforce the benefits of social and therapeutic horticulture in improving well-being and mental health and we see ourselves reflected throughout this excellent publication.

However, it is important to recognise that horticulture is not always an idyllic pastime. Statistics show that the suicide rates among farmers and growers are just as high as in any other industry. The pressures and stress caused by targets and competition are just as high in rural industries as in any other areas of work, and unless both rural and urban industries can address the issues of stress and pressure in the workplace, the incidence of mental illness will only continue to increase. This is something we must never forget.

We warmly welcome the publication of this guide, which we would have found extremely useful when we first started out. We hope it will inspire the creation of many more projects in the future that work towards caring for people and caring for plants for the benefit of the vulnerable, excluded and forgotten members of our communities.

Jessica Davies, Manager,
Sheltered Work Opportunities Project,
Cherry Tree Nursery, Bournemouth

Acknowledgements

This guide was prepared by the Research Team at Loughborough University as part of the 'Growing Together' project funded by the National Lottery Community Fund (now the Big Lottery Fund). 'Growing Together – Promoting Social Inclusion, Health and Well-being for Vulnerable Adults through the use of Horticulture and Gardening' is a collaboration between Loughborough University and the charity Thrive.

The authors would like to acknowledge the Big Lottery Fund for the financial support of this project under grant number RG 10024093.

The authors acknowledge the cooperation and collaboration of their colleagues at Thrive, especially Tim Spurgeon and Louise Finnis and the consultants to the project: John Ferris, Carol Norman, Bill Silburn and Linda Eggins.

The authors would also like to thank the following individuals for providing information, help and advice. Without them this guide would not have been possible:

Sam Anderson, Chris Balchin, Richard Clare, John Cliff, Sarah Corps, Jessica Davies, Arn de Bock, Eve Dracup, Darrell Evans, Fi Garrard, Paula Gent, Angela Grey-Lake, Jenny Grut, Mike Hamilton, Ron Howson, Aloysius Laloo, Sandra Morland, Ian Pepperdine, Den Phillips, Linda Phillips, Sheila Richards, Keri Schofield, Bobbi Smith, Roger Smith, Ian Sutcliffe, Sue Tabor, Paul Tomlin, Lyn Townsend, Tim Wright. Our grateful thanks also to all other project staff who provided such invaluable support.

Thanks also to the following projects for their help:

Bridewell Organic Gardens, Care Co-ops Community Farm, Charnwood Gardening Project, Cherry Tree Nursery, Coach House Trust, CRT Allotment, Horticulture Skills Training, Cwmbran Countryside Team, Earthworks St Albans, Fairwater Community Garden Project, First Step, Gamelea Countryside Training Trust, Greenfingers, Green Health Partnership, Heeley City Farm, Horticare, Inishfree, Moss Allotment Garden Project, Natural Growth Project, Redhall Walled Garden, Roots and Shoots, Shaw Trust Richmond Park Project, The Northcliffe Project, Trunkwell Garden Project, Unstone Grange Organic Gardens.

1 Introduction

Introduction

Purpose of the guide

The purpose of this guide is to highlight issues of social inclusion among practitioners of social and therapeutic horticulture and to illustrate ways in which horticulture and gardening projects can promote it. The guide also looks at issues such as the effective management of social and therapeutic horticulture (STH) projects for a range of vulnerable groups (for example, those with learning difficulties, mental health problems, physical health problems and disabilities). However, it is not intended as a prescriptive guide or as a code of conduct. Not all STH projects will choose to adopt the systems and processes referred to in this guide. For example, some project organisers may consider quality assurance systems too bureaucratic or prescribed for their purposes. Projects are free to adopt the management system and style that works best for them, but this guide should provide even the most free-spirited of gardeners with some ideas for practice or development.

Furthermore, the purpose of this guide is not to serve as a manual of horticultural therapy, horticulture or gardening, but to provide directions for STH practitioners to identify and locate additional information and training in these subjects. Details of training are provided throughout the guide and Appendix B, for example, lists some publications in those fields that will be of assistance to practitioners. Appendix B also includes details of publications that will be particularly useful in the teaching of therapeutic horticulture at certificate and diploma level. Appendix C lists the contact details of some useful organisations. While this list is not exhaustive, those organisations included will also provide a gateway to other relevant agencies and information.

While this guide has been written for all of those working in social and therapeutic horticulture, those practitioners who are relatively new to the field or are contemplating managing or organising a STH project in the future should find the guide particularly useful (see Appendix A, which provides a simple checklist for new practitioners).

There has been a debate among practitioners as to what constitutes STH. Some have argued that this should be limited to those activities and procedures that are purely horticultural, that is, only those that involve plant care or propagation. Others have taken a wider view and have included all those activities that are associated with the garden project including design, landscaping, construction, art and craft. We have adopted an inclusive approach as the design, construction and maintenance of a garden require many different actions and skills and it is difficult to separate horticultural activities and experiences from many related ones.

Do the benefits of gardening arise, for example, from the handling of plants, the garden landscape, the knowledge and satisfaction of having laid out the flower beds and lawns or having constructed a shed for gardeners to shelter in? All of these (and more) are probably involved. Indeed, many of those who attend projects call themselves 'gardeners' even if their work is confined to laying slabs or other construction. Their environment is the garden and their work serves to enhance it.

This guide examines some of the processes that are at the heart of gardening projects and that contribute to their success, for example, the management and finances of a project, the variety of activities on offer, the involvement of clients with the management of the project and so on. Evidence and ideas are drawn from research data obtained during the Growing Together study of STH in the UK and by consultation with the charity Thrive and with practitioners working in the field.

Growing Together research programme

The Growing Together study was the first detailed investigation of STH in the UK. It was carried out in association with the charity Thrive (formerly known as the Society for Horticultural Therapy), which is the leading organisation in the UK promoting the use of horticulture for training, therapy, employment and health. Thrive coordinates a national network of projects in addition to running its own training and therapeutic gardens. The research was funded by the National Lottery's Community Fund (now the Big Lottery Fund) and started in June 2002. The final report *Health, well-being and social inclusion* is being published alongside this guide.

The first phase of the study was an extensive review of the literature on STH, which was published in Spring 2003. This showed that while there was an abundance of articles and books of a general nature on the subject, there was a shortage of actual data and evidence. What little evidence there was, however, suggested that horticulture projects could provide benefits in health and well-being for a wide range of vulnerable people and in many different contexts. It also suggested that such projects could promote social inclusion, which has become a significant aspect of the current government's health and social care policy.

The second phase of the study constituted a survey of gardening and horticulture projects. Almost 900 projects responded to the survey, which provided information about the size and funding of projects, the number of clients, percentages of women and minority ethnic clients, numbers of project staff and their qualifications, aims and perceived benefits. It enabled the researchers to assess the scale of activity in the area and to visualise the context in which horticulture projects operate. This information has been used in the preparation of this guide.

The third part of the study focused on 25 individual projects, their clients and staff. More than 200 people were interviewed, including clients, staff, carers and family members and project activities were observed and analysed. Additionally, health professionals – mental health practitioners, occupational therapists, general practitioners and others – were interviewed in order to collate information about referral procedures. The benefits to clients were analysed in terms of proposed key dimensions of social inclusion, namely, production, consumption, social interaction and engagement with the political system. Results show that horticulture and gardening projects do indeed promote social inclusion in the areas outlined above. For example, many of those who we interviewed during the course of the research described their activity at projects as meaningful work rather than as therapy; they valued the opportunity to be productive; they were able to access some goods and services directly as a result of participating in projects; they had made friends and acquaintances at garden projects and regarded them as an important arena for social contact and they had had involvement in the running of their projects. These issues are discussed in this guide in the context of the activities and management of the projects. A detailed analysis of the results of the Growing Together research is published in the final report. Verbatim quotes from interviews recorded as part of that study are used in this guide but names have been changed to protect anonymity.

From social exclusion towards inclusion

In recent years, in the study of deprivation and vulnerability the emphasis has shifted from issues of 'poverty' to 'social exclusion'. Poverty and social exclusion are not the same. While poverty is about the distribution of resources, or access to them, social exclusion is about the ability to play a part in society and the community and to share in its benefits and opportunities as well as contribute to its richness. Clearly, poverty plays a role in social exclusion but is only one of many factors. Social exclusion is a multidimensional problem.

The present government was instrumental in setting up a Social Exclusion Unit in 1997 to address the issue. The Unit defined social exclusion as:

> ... a shorthand term for what can happen when people or areas suffer from a combination of linked problems such as unemployment, poor skills, low incomes, poor housing, high crime environments, bad health and family breakdown.

However, while such a definition outlines the problem it does not explain the underlying mechanisms or processes and there have been many attempts to define social exclusion and to produce theoretical frameworks and models. Some researchers have approached the issue from the perspective of work and employment and have, for example, viewed work as an integrative factor that positions an individual within society.

Others have examined the responsibilities and role of the state and the individual and have looked at family and community networks. These and many other approaches have helped policy makers to understand why individuals, groups of people and areas are excluded.

In this guide we use a particular model of social exclusion that proposes four key dimensions[1]. This model is useful for our purposes because it can readily be applied to the type of activities and processes seen at horticulture projects.

The four key dimensions of inclusion – production, consumption, social interaction and political engagement – are described as follows:

* Production is the notion of being engaged in a meaningful and socially valuable activity that can include paid employment, education or training, or unpaid or voluntary work.
* Consumption is the idea of being able to buy the goods and services that other people can buy, and to access the types of public services that other people can access.
* Social interaction refers to social networks and cultural identity, having access and opportunities to mix and engage with other people.
* Political engagement broadly refers to the process of self-determination, that is, 'having a say' in what happens and how a community or organisation is run. This may take many forms, from active participation in the party political process through to involvement in the running of a club, organisation or group. It may be formal and involve committees or be casual and rely on ad hoc gatherings or partnerships.

Some of these processes may occur naturally at garden projects. For example, most projects provide an opportunity for social contact that occurs with little need for encouragement or intervention from project organisers. Other dimensions may require more careful orchestration or planning, for example, involving clients in the running of the project in a meaningful way.

Future research

The Growing Together study would not have been possible without the help and cooperation of the projects that completed the questionnaire and those members of clients, members of staff and volunteers who took part in interviews. Research evidence helps to shape both policy and practice. This is particularly important in respect of STH, which is gaining prominence in the field of conventional health and social care.

---

[1] Burchardt, T., Le Grand, J. and Piachaud, D. (2002) 'Degrees of exclusion: developing a dynamic, multidimensional measure', in J. Hills, J. Le Grand and D. Piachaud (eds) *Understanding social exclusion*, New York, NY: Oxford University Press, pp 30-43.

There will always be a need for research evidence, and project managers and volunteers can play a key role in accumulating data by continuing to participate in research and where possible by carrying out their own research. Involvement in research not only helps to build a body of knowledge that forms the foundation for the subject but it also stimulates interest in the theoretical aspects of the subjects and, therefore, personal development. Where projects carry out their own research, even if this is done on a small scale, the findings should be disseminated beyond the project members where appropriate. Publications in magazines and newsletters, and presentations and talks at local meetings and seminars are all effective ways of ensuring that such findings reach a wider audience. Organisations such as Thrive and Cultivations (see Appendix C) organise meetings where projects can present information about their work. Results from research are always welcome.

A note on terminology

To avoid any confusion or ambiguity, the term 'client' is used throughout this guide to refer to an intended beneficiary of the project for whom a fee is usually paid. Clients are generally referred to projects by social services departments or health trusts but occasionally they present themselves at projects and pay their own fees.

'Volunteer' is used to describe an unpaid helper whose function is to assist in the maintenance of the garden or project site, or to facilitate the clients in their work. Some volunteers are engaged in both of these roles, but others carry out maintenance or administrative tasks and have little or no contact with clients.

Although the distinction between 'client' and 'volunteer' seems, at first sight, to be clear, the boundaries are blurred. Many of those who offer their services as volunteers also have significant health and social needs. They take the opportunity to engage in an activity that they perceive to be both helpful (to the project) and therapeutic (to themselves). Some projects do not make any particular distinction between clients and volunteers and treat them equally when allocating tasks and activities and when offering feedback and advice. Others are mindful of the fact that clients have been referred to them by health and welfare agencies, which pay a fee for project services. These projects then provide specific activities and assessments of their clients and use their volunteers to assist them in that process. The use of terminology may also blur the boundaries between the roles of clients and volunteers; for example, some projects refer to their clients as 'volunteers' and find alternative terms to describe their unpaid helpers, such as 'volunteer officers'.

The complexities of terminology and client/volunteer/service user definitions are summarised in the following quotation from the organiser of a large nursery project for people with mental health problems:

"When we first started, the people who set it up called us the volunteer/clients. And they said, 'We don't like being called clients. We're coming here as volunteers, of our own free will, we don't have to come here if we don't want to. So, we're volunteers, please.' And so we've always called them volunteers since, so therefore any volunteers/helpers that came to help had to be called 'friends', really, because we don't confuse the two, although the borders are very tight sometimes. I mean, most of the people who come in as friends actually really could qualify as volunteers and some people who come as volunteers feel that they could just be helpers really ... there isn't much borderline between the two, really."

Terminology adopted by projects should be chosen with care and project organisers should be aware that different projects may assign different definitions to the terms used.

Although we refer to the field as STH, many of those working at the projects would prefer not to use the word 'therapy' to describe their activities as this gives a medical context to the tasks rather than a work-orientated one. If the aim of the project is to provide something that is 'a bit like work' and has its associated benefits then for the participants to be constantly reminded that they are clients or service users and that they are at their therapy is counter-productive.

"Everybody that comes here calls this their 'work', and I quite like to encourage that idea, that it's work and that they're capable of doing work, ... I would hate to think that somebody was saying, 'Oh, I'm going to my therapy', because it's like an extension of their illness, if you like, as opposed to being a way forward from their illness.... I'm not denying that it isn't therapeutic, it probably is, but people's perception of what they're doing when they come here is that it's their work." (project organiser)

2 Activities and opportunities

Activities and opportunities

The clients

STH projects provide a service for many different client groups. The figures in Table 1 are taken from the national survey of projects. Only 35.5% of the projects worked with only one client group, the rest had clients from more than one group and almost half (46.4%) worked with clients from three groups or more. Working with a mixed group of clients did not appear to cause any particular problems. Indeed, there are some advantages in that it presents opportunities for people with a range of health or care needs to help each other.

Although projects tended to focus on a specific client group, for example, people with learning difficulties, they frequently accepted clients with other problems. People with learning difficulties or mental health problems were generally referred to projects by local health and social care agencies (for example, social services or community mental health teams).

In some cases practitioners from statutory health services, usually occupational therapists, were instrumental in organising and implementing STH projects at their hospitals or centres.

Few STH projects provide a service for women-only groups and fewer still have significant participation by people from black and minority ethnic groups. Information from the survey also shows that only around 30% of the total users of projects were women and that 6% of all clients came from black and minority ethnic communities.

There are a number of possible reasons for this under-representation. For example, horticulture and gardening have not always been successfully promoted among these groups. Cultural barriers are also present. Research from the Growing Together study shows that women from some minority ethnic groups experience difficulties in accessing leisure opportunities outside the home. Another barrier is the lack of information about the number of people from black and minority ethnic groups in the local community. These issues need to be addressed both by further research and by action from projects themselves.

Table 1: Client groups using STH projects

Client group	% of projects providing a service for that client group[a]
Learning difficulties	48.7
Mental health needs	40.6
Challenging behaviour	17.2
Physical disabilities	16.9
Unemployed	13.9
Multiple disabilities	11.7
Young people	10.9
Older people	10.6
Low income	9.3
Drug and alcohol misuse	8.9
Rehabilitation	7.2
Accident/illness	6.0
Visually impaired	5.4
Offenders	5.1
Hearing impaired	4.7
Black and minority ethnic	4.3
Ex-offenders	3.7
Major illness	3.6
Homeless and vulnerable housed	2.4
Women-only groups	2.4
Refugees/asylum seekers	1.1

Note: [a] Where representation by that group is approximately 20% or more of the people attending.

There are a number of ways to increase participation among these groups, including specific promotion strategies targeted at under-represented groups. In one project, positive discrimination is practised in that women clients are taken preferentially to men so that representation becomes equal. Some projects have introduced women-only days. Other approaches include dedicated promotional strategies among black and minority ethnic communities as well as ensuring that project information and other printed material are translated into relevant languages.

Research suggests that dedicated projects can be beneficial for clients in a number of ways. Women-only wilderness groups in the US, for example, have proved effective in reinforcing solidarity among women, providing women with safe and protected environments in which to socialise, engage in outdoor activity and avoid discrimination. Similar benefits have been recorded among STH projects in the UK for women and for black and minority ethnic groups.

When asked about what she gained from attending a women-only gardening group for women from black and minority ethnic communities, one woman explained:

> "We can talk easily, we can, jokes about it, everything, because in our culture, we can't make any jokes in front of the males. Because [we] enjoy ourselves, we can just talk, talking and, give ideas, get ideas…. Well, in our community, most the woman stays at home. And, we were asking womens come out and talking there, because most of the womans have been not allowed to go out work with the male, go and work, and do something with the males."

Regardless of whether STH projects are aimed specifically at people with mental health problems, learning difficulties or at other socially excluded groups, it is important that all projects address issues of race and gender by ensuring women and black and minority ethnic clients are represented equally, recognising factors that may contribute to under-representation and take positive action to counter this.

The Black Environment Network (BEN), the Women's Environmental Network (WEN) and Thrive can be useful as sources of information and support for projects seeking to increase the involvement of women and black and minority ethnic groups.

BEN (www.ben-network.org.uk) was established "to promote equality of opportunity with respect to ethnic communities in the preservation protection and development of the environment". Their work is aimed at integrating "social, cultural and environmental concerns in the context of sustainable development". They work across 'diverse sectors' on issues such as the natural environment, the built environment, heritage, social justice, health and housing.

WEN (www.wen.org.uk) is a campaigning organisation, "which represents women and campaigns on issues, which link women, environment and health".

Involvement in decision making

Many clients benefit from being involved in project decision-making processes as it helps them to feel included and that their contributions count and can make a difference. Some projects introduce formal meetings or set up client/volunteer committees so that clients can have their say and be represented in respect of future plans and how projects are organised and run. At one project for people with mental health problems, all clients (there are more than a 100 of them) are given the opportunity to represent the client group on the project committee on a rotational basis. Minutes of these meetings are recorded and stored on the project's files. A client explains:

> "I like to feel needed myself, and obviously they do, and it's nice to be able to see each person knowing a little bit about different things and then when the meetings come up everyone puts it together; and we take it in turns to chair the meetings which gives people a little bit more responsibility, a chance to discuss things and put things forward, which I think is really good because it gives a kind of a level, a one sort of level for everyone, because each person is contributing in some sort of way, whether it be knowledge or work or whatever."

Summary

Think of strategic ways of ensuring equality of opportunity and representation (for example, women-only days, promotion work in black and minority ethnic communities).

Consult and make links with relevant agencies and organisations, such as BEN and WEN.

Ensure clients have access to a range of activities and opportunities that promote social inclusion and generate positive health and well-being outcomes.

Help clients become more independent and to make progress in terms of social, cognitive and education/employment skills where appropriate.

Ensure opportunities for clients are based on assessment of their needs and wishes and that opportunities and activities are meaningful and rewarding.

Give clients opportunities for engaging in decision-making processes through project committee meetings and so on.

Project activities

The extent and diversity of gardening, horticultural and other activities across STH projects are considerable. Many of these cannot be described simply as gardening jobs (for example, digging beds, cultivating, planting, propagating, weeding) but include many other activities such as construction (of sheds, polytunnels and other structures), hard landscaping, laying slabs, conservation (of woodland and wildlife) and even arts and craft work.

However, all of these aspects of STH activity offer clients opportunities to undertake new and different physical tasks and to develop their skills. Pricking out, propagating, watering, weeding and so on all offer clients the ability to work with their hands and to increase physical ability, such as fine motor skills or joint flexibility. Other activities require strategic skills, for example, planning and laying out flower and vegetable beds.

Outdoor crafts can be part of 'garden work' ... wood turning using pole lathes has experienced a recent revival. They are relatively easy to construct and can be used to turn some very intricate and high quality pieces. Many other crafts are practised, including black smithery and outdoor firing of pottery.

Some projects with specific objectives, for example, employment skills training, have a dedicated programme of activities planned in order to meet formal training requirements. Other projects gear their activities around the individual needs of clients but also with project sustainability in mind. For example, one gardening project aimed at supporting people with severe learning difficulties offers one-to-one support for clients and recognises that some clients will only be able to undertake limited gardening jobs, but that being outside and working alongside others in a team are the main benefits to those clients. However, in order to sustain and promote the project, contract work is undertaken (in and around the local community) and plant sales are held. Where there is a shortfall in productivity (among clients who are unable to work consistently), volunteers help out, particularly during times of high demand (in late spring, for example, when plant sales take place).

Not all project work and activity takes place outdoors. Naturally, a big part of project activity takes place in greenhouses, polytunnels and potting sheds. However, many projects also offer dry spaces for clients to participate in arts and craft work, for example, and these often run concurrently with other activities. Around 20% of projects have dedicated facilities for arts and crafts. Most project activity also offers clients opportunities to work alongside others and to form new friendships and associations.

Arts and crafts are used in many different ways to decorate and brighten up the gardens.

©John Ferris

A tea break provides a useful opportunity to develop friendships.

One project, for example, has a dedicated craft cabin for clients who do not want to participate in outdoor gardening work but prefer to stay indoors together and participate in craft work, such as flower pressing and making pictures from materials they have collected on site. This aspect of project activity has developed over the years to such an extent that a dedicated arts and crafts officer has been employed, on a part-time basis, to instruct clients and to help them make their own greetings cards (using materials from the site), which the project then sells to the general public.

Visiting artists and craftspeople often bring new skills and knowledge to a project. A local willow sculptor helped clients to produce their own sculptures at this project.

A diverse and interesting range of unusual activities also takes place on many project sites. For example, one organic gardening project designed and constructed a lavender labyrinth on site. Another project, for people with mental health problems, brought in a willow sculptor who helped clients produce their own structures as well as producing other work, such as a working pole lathe. The benefits to clients of undertaking this type of work can be many; they can help those clients with mental illness focus on physical activity (as a way of diverting attention from their mental health problems) and producing objects of beauty. They can also be restorative and aid relaxation as well as help to emphasise clients' abilities, thus

Many projects have dedicated facilities for indoor art and craft activities and these are also popular with clients.

shifting attention away from their illness or disability (this is true for many clients with learning difficulties who, in day care facilities for example, are not always empowered to work or undertake independent activity).

It is worth remembering that although a large number of projects offer a range of diverse and sometimes unusual activities, in many cases clients enjoy undertaking quite basic gardening and related work. Here a client explains why he simply enjoys sowing seeds and watching plants grow:

Watching plants grow offers endless fascination to people of all abilities. The photograph below, was taken by a client with learning difficulties and chosen as one of his favourite photographs.

"I think it's just, like, to see it progress, really. You know, starting off with, like, a bag, you know, a packet of seeds, and, erm, seeing the end results and having the end results on the, erm, table, usually to eat. But it's nice to see it because, you know, because nature's an amazing thing, isn't it? And, erm, just to see something start from seed and then grow into a, you know, something you can eat, is quite amazing."

Evidence from environmental psychology shows that the natural setting is a key dimension of the 'restorative environment', and data from our research shows that many clients, like the one above, value being able to watch the process of growth and to have the opportunity to assist it. Being closer to, or directly involved, in the natural environment is an important aspect of social and therapeutic horticulture and many clients are encouraged to commune not just with each other, but also with nature and its restorative opportunities.

Being able to enjoy and participate in meditative or reflexive activity that requires nothing more than a safe or quiet garden space to sit and relax are important aspects of STH. To give an example here, one project, for people with mental health problems, encouraged clients to become involved in all aspects of nursery activity, from propagation to producing plants for sale in the nursery shop. While clients clearly enjoyed 'watching things grow' and watching their plants being sold to paying customers, they also equally enjoyed the opportunity to use the dedicated, enclosed, quiet spaces for them to sit and enjoy the fruits of their labours. This particular project had also constructed a memorial garden in memory of a project member who had died.

A memorial garden at a large commercial project provides a space for peace and reflection. Memorials to past colleagues can take many different forms.

Meaningful activities: common goals and purposes

Many different tasks are necessary to maintain and improve a garden or project site. The tasks are interrelated and have a purpose and coherence that is usually clearly visible or can easily be explained, for example, weeding a flower bed or vegetable patch enhances its aesthetic appeal, sowing seeds or planting seedlings ensures a crop will be available for harvesting, building a shed provides shelter for the gardeners and security for the tools and so on. However, the purpose of some tasks may not be so clear, particularly some of those related to commercial enterprises or larger-scale production. These may require explanation. Tasks should always be meaningful and purposeful. Having a common purpose helps to bring the group together and activities that require a joint effort can be particularly fruitful. Recent research has shown that working together as a team can promote a greater feeling of happiness than individual working. When a major task is required it can be used to provide a sense of occasion, to unite the project members as a team....

> "Well, usually, if it's a hard work, there's a big group of people all doing it at the same time, like moving logs around [...] these logs here, and so, it's quite, quite nice doing hard work with other people."

Here, although the task could have been carried out by individuals working alone over a greater period of time, the cooperative aspects would have been missed.

Activities can be chosen to suit a client's abilities, preferences and temperament. Clients, too, will suggest activities that may be important to them or that they would like to try. These will vary from small changes in current activities such as growing a new variety of plant to larger-scale projects, for example, creating a new garden feature.

Not all garden activities involve ambitious projects or heavy work, just sowing seeds and watching them grow is the basic foundation of all gardening.... "... just to see something start from seed...".

Sometimes attempting the difficult or seemingly impossible shows that many things are achievable if you have a go ... like the construction of this 'henge':

"Let's do it, let's try it. You know, trying something difficult, that looks difficult or impossible. These people have been told for years, 'Oh, you're ill, you can't do that'."

Opportunities for clients

STH projects provide a range of opportunities for clients to engage in activities that promote social inclusion and produce benefits in health and well-being. Further, this is a two-way process in that projects themselves – the management team or organisers – can benefit from client involvement in decision-making processes and meetings and discussions about how the project is managed and plans for the future.

In most cases, STH projects aim to extend clients' social networks, foster independence, responsibility and inclusion as well as offer skills through education and employment training.

It is important that the type of activity individual clients engage in is appropriate (in terms of their abilities and understanding) and based on an assessment of their needs and requirements as well as on client choice. It is the responsibility of project organisers, who also have knowledge and understanding of project objectives, to assign tasks and activities that incorporate both their assessment of the individual client's needs and their choices and preferences.

Miles from the sea? Two examples of beach gardens – the construction of features such as these generates interest and enthusiasm and enables skills such as garden design to be learned and practiced. Funding is often available for 'mini-projects' and they are 'reversible' if the land is needed for a new project.

In some cases, for example, where clients have severe learning difficulties, assessments will be informed by input from other health and social care professionals, relatives and carers and by monitoring individual progress. Some clients, while enjoying access to a range of activities at projects, may not be physically able to do many of them. However, most projects offer opportunities for clients to participate in activities that suit their needs

while at the same time promoting social inclusion by integrating clients within the project team as a whole and in local communities.

At one project (for people with learning difficulties), all clients are offered the opportunity to participate in contract work, which involves them going off site as a team to work on gardening contracts for local businesses and charities. Here they strim verges, mow lawns and do some weeding with supervision from project organisers. This type of off-site activity gives them the opportunity to travel, engage in physical activity, work as a team, operate machinery and meet people in the local community. Few of these opportunities are available at day care centres or in institutions. However, some of the project's clients choose never to go off site or, indeed, work outside in the gardens or in the greenhouses and potting sheds but decide to stay inside in the craft cabin working with others on producing, for example, greetings cards and pressing flowers. The objective of most projects is to offer clients a choice about what they do when they attend.

The wide range of activities on offer means that many clients will be able to participate in activities not available to them elsewhere. One project organiser explained that most of their clients (people with learning difficulties), in day centres, were not allowed to make a cup of tea on their own but at the gardening project were encouraged (while supervised) to operate machinery and tools, for example, strimmers, lawn mowers and power tools. Unusual activities, for example, making willow sculptures, using a pottery kiln, constructing a beach house, are also activities in which many clients would not participate in their daily lives.

A key aspect of STH is that it helps to foster independence by teaching life skills and providing new opportunities for clients to develop new skills and build self-confidence. Most projects, for example, require clients to travel some distance to and from the project site. Travel arrangements often involve clients travelling away from their homes or social care institutions. While these arrangements are often organised for the clients by project staff, many clients develop their self-confidence and independence through the use of public transport.

Individual plots can take many different forms and give clients a sense of pride and ownership.

Other ways clients benefit in terms of their independence and self-esteem is by undertaking new activities, in particular developing their horticultural or gardening skills. Some clients may already have an interest in gardening, while others may be new to it. However, research from the Growing Together study has shown that most clients benefit from undertaking activities such as cultivating plants, helping to construct garden features, digging borders and 'watching things grow'. For some these activities can be beneficial physically, that is, they provide opportunities to become physically more active and agile. While for

others, gardening provides relaxation and opportunities to be reflective and enjoy the outdoors. It is important that, whatever type of work clients undertake at projects, this is meaningful and rewarding for them.

Formal training and qualifications

Around a quarter of projects provide accredited training, mostly in land-based subjects, including horticulture and crafts such as woodwork. Courses such as those leading to National Vocational Qualifications (NVQs) and ones accredited by the National Proficiency Tests Council (NPTC) and the National Open College Network (NOCN) are offered. Some projects have ceased their involvement in this training because of perceived difficulties with documentation; however, those projects that continue to provide training report that accreditation bodies and moderators are helpful and supportive and that the system for obtaining accreditation to teach and assess the courses is not too onerous.

Projects provide both informal and accredited training such as NPTC qualifications. 'Folder work' is popular among many different groups of clients.

Results from the survey of projects show that clients with learning difficulties are the largest group involved in accredited training. It is likely that this particular group may reap the greatest benefits since few of the clients have any qualifications on entry to the projects. A formal teaching programme provides good indicators of progress and evidence of achievement. This is not only useful when moving from the project to other training or employment, but it also engenders a sense of satisfaction and success and is greatly valued by the clients.

Details about accreditation and courses from:	Website address
National Open College Network	www.nocn.org.uk/
National Proficiency Tests Council	www.nptc.org.uk/
National Vocational Qualifications	www.dfes.gov.uk/nvq/
The Award Scheme Development and Accreditation Network (ASDAN)	www.asdan.co.uk/

Summary

Offer a range of activities for clients.

Assess the needs and wishes of clients in respect of the type of activities in which they wish to participate.

Provide meaningful activities and explain the purpose of tasks.

Bring in outside expertise where appropriate.

Offer clients opportunities to be reflective and enjoy the restorative benefits of project activities.

Team work and cooperation are beneficial and work can be organised to include them.

Offer specific skills and training as required and consider providing accredited training if appropriate.

The benefits of work

There has been a great deal of research on the benefits of work and on the impact of unemployment on mental health. Financial remuneration is not the only reward of work. A study carried out in the 1950s (Morse and Weiss, 1955[2]) showed that most people would still go to work even if they had enough money to live comfortably without working. When the study was repeated 25 years later the results were similar, although the percentage who would remain at work had fallen slightly, from 80% in the 1950s to 72% in 1980. Most people gain a number of benefits (listed below) as a result of employment, in addition to financial ones. Unemployment can often lead to negative psychological effects and sometimes serious mental health problems and many people with mental health problems have difficulties in finding employment. Without employment some people are affected by a loss of structure from their lives, experience diminished access to social networks and a reduced status or sense of purpose. They can also be at risk of social exclusion.

Although there is still some debate surrounding this issue, a number of work-related factors is seen as important. These can be listed as follows:

* availability of money
* imposition of a time structure on the working day
* regular shared experience and contact outside the nuclear family
* linking of individuals to goals and purposes
* personal status and identity
* enforcing of activity
* opportunity for control
* opportunity for skill use

---

[2]   Morse, N.C. and Weiss, R.S. (1955) 'The function and meaning of work and the job', *American Sociological Review*, vol 20, pp 191-8.

- variety of activities
- physical security.

These factors all relate to the dimensions of social inclusion mentioned earlier. Although they can be seen as primarily contributing to the dimension of 'production', work-related factors are involved in the other dimensions. For example, work can offer the opportunity for clients to feel more in control of their environment and have a greater input into the decision-making process.

A structure to the working day

For many clients, projects provide a structured routine for their daily lives – they frequently report that projects give them 'something to get out of bed for'. Over 70% of projects are open for three or more days each week and the average attendance is three days per week. Such attendance helps to establish a routine and where possible clients should be encouraged to attend regularly. Sporadic visits to a project or short sessions, while they may be enjoyable, are unlikely to create the necessary routine. Routine is of particular importance for those individuals who are progressing towards employment, and lack of a 'work habit' or 'work discipline' has been blamed for the difficulties that some clients experience in keeping their jobs once they have found paid employment.

Although most projects are open for three days a week or more, some are only able to open for one or two days because of staff shortages or lack of resources. Ways of extending the project opening time can be explored – perhaps forming a partnership with other projects or organisations. Also, depending on the aims of the project, if the project has a large number of clients who attend infrequently, reducing the number of clients and increasing their attendance may be a preferred option.

Personal status

Projects help to promote self-confidence and self-esteem and can enable clients to see themselves as 'workers' or 'gardeners' rather than as patients or clients attending therapy sessions.

"... it gave me an identity, a new identity, because now I could think of myself as a gardener. Otherwise I was just a patient, somebody who suffers from a mental illness. And through coming to the garden, I was a gardener, and if people asked me what I did, there wasn't the usual awkward silence while I tried to think how to put it, but I could say that I was a gardener and talk about what I'd been doing that day." (project client with mental health problems)

Training, the acquisition of skills and qualifications, all serve to enhance this sense of personal status. The use of specialised tools and machinery helps to increase self-esteem and defines the person as a skilled man or woman. It is also empowering as many clients have been denied the opportunity to use tools, for example, those living in residential accommodation may not have access to gardening or other tools. Some may have been specifically prevented from using tools or items considered dangerous to them. Clients often find the use of strimmers, mowers and other garden equipment to be particularly enjoyable. Proper training enables tools and machinery to be used safely and engenders a sense of achievement.

Tools and machinery, such as lawnmowers and strimmers can help to define the user as a skilled person.

The use of terminology has been discussed earlier in this guide. It, too, has an impact on clients' self-esteem and sense of status. It is important to use terms with which clients feel comfortable and which help to promote their self-confidence and sense of inclusion rather than those which highlight their dependence or disability.

Attendance and commitment to a project can be strengthened by a contract or agreement with the client. Some projects offer such a contract. This sets out the commitments of the client to the project and vice versa. Such formal arrangements help to make project attendance feel 'more like work'.

Appropriate productivity

While clients and project organisers value daily structure and routine, they acknowledge that the pressure on clients and expectations of productivity are low. The 'right amount' of pressure is necessary – enough to provide structure and routine, engagement with the project and the encouragement to be active but not so much as to cause stress to the clients. Achieving the right balance is important as clients report the favourable effects of both *lack of pressure* and *daily routine.* The structure and organisation of the working day can be used to provide the balance and can be tailored according to the needs of individuals. On most projects the working day for the clients starts at around 9.30-10.00 and ends at around 15.30-16.00. While this may be suitable for most clients, some may wish to work a longer day. Some projects enable clients to work longer hours by giving them specific tasks that can be carried out prior to the beginning of the official day, for example, giving them responsibility for tidying a part of the site or for preparing tools and materials for the other clients. Such an arrangement can be useful provided that there is adequate supervision.

Summary

Routine and structure are important for many clients and regular attendance should be encouraged.

Participation in projects can be used to enhance clients' sense of personal status and self-esteem.

The use of tools and machinery can also help to increase self-esteem.

Clients should be facilitated to provide an appropriate level of productivity.

Moving on

In most cases, the client's stay at a project is intended to be finite. It is a stage in their rehabilitation or training and the expectation is that eventually they will move on to employment, further training or different activities. Some projects offer a fixed period of training, for example, a two-year course to obtain NPTC or NVQ qualifications. In these cases, funding arrangements may not allow the clients to stay longer and they have to move in any case to make way for the next intake. Other projects are able to offer the client an unlimited stay. On average, clients stay at a project for around three years. However, some will be unable to find employment or places in education and may stay for much longer. It is not unusual to find clients who have been at projects for 10 years or more. Although attending the project may itself be an enjoyable activity, there is a need for clients to experience progress and the feeling of 'moving on', even if they do not leave the project for a number of years.

Physically moving on allows new clients to join a project and for it to remain a vibrant and interesting place.

Progress within a project may take many forms, for example, an improvement in health, well-being and self-confidence; the development of social and communication skills; acquisition of life skills to enable independent living or travel; formal qualifications or specific training. A process of assessment will enable both the client and the project organiser to see the progress and will allow the project staff to gauge the effectiveness of their activities. Goals, for clients, provide a direction for

Contract work takes the clients off site and may be used as part of a pathway of progression.

them to progress towards and a marker against which to measure progress. Some clients will have a clear idea of what they would like to achieve at the project (and beyond), while others will be unsure and need assistance in defining what it is that they actually want from the project.

Assessment and outcomes

The overall purpose of assessment is to provide project staff with the right information so that they can facilitate the progress of a client towards their chosen goals and ambitions, or to address any particular issues that have been identified. This general purpose can be broken down into a number of specific points. Assessment, therefore, can help to:

- determine general areas of ability and set a baseline from which a relevant training programme can be implemented;
- facilitate the work of staff by providing information towards developing an appropriate therapy programme;
- assess and monitor levels of progress and identify areas for clients' development;
- identify the level of staff support required;
- highlight 'gaps' in knowledge or previous training;
- identify and plan the use of specific methods or equipment to overcome physical limitations;
- identify changes over time or patterns in the way an activity is undertaken;
- avoid the dangers of a person being selected because of their ability to do a job (which implies that production is more important than individual development); this may be particularly important in projects involved in commercial activity or production;

- assist staff in preparation of individual care plans;
- enable decisions to be made on the basis of evidence, rather than impressions. (Adapted and abridged from McChesney, 1994, whose article 'Assessment' is available from Thrive, as Briefing Sheet[3], number 208.)

ASSESSMENT SHEET

Skill: *UPPER LIMB STRENGTH/HAND FUNCTIONS*

Activity: *WATERING A POT PLANT*

Activity Component	Date							
Acknowledge instructions								
OPEN RIGHT HAND								
GRASP EMPTY CAN (RIGHT HAND)								
GRASP TAP WITH LEFT HAND								
TURN TAP, FILL CAN								
TURN TAP OFF								
CARRY CAN TO PLANT								
TIP CAN AND WATER PLANT								
PLACE CAN ON FLOOR.								
concentration span (gd, pr, av)								

Fill box with: 0 = no response at all   ✸ WITH ASSISTANCE
                         1 = tried and nearly succeeded
                         2 = achieved skill

Comments and Date:

There is no standardised assessment system and no single method that is applicable to all client groups and all situations. Some projects use assessment sheets that have been developed from occupational therapy practice. These grade and record the performance of the client in specific tasks and their psychological attitude to those tasks and to the project in general. Such assessments are particularly useful to monitor progress, for example, of clients with learning difficulties or those recovering from injury or stroke. Some project workers have used their training in occupational therapy to develop such assessment methods and information is available from textbooks in occupational therapy. Projects are also willing to share information on methods that they use and being part of a network can be beneficial in this respect. Evaluation of specific tasks can also prove useful during the process of risk assessment – the client's ability to carry out tasks safely can be assessed alongside other criteria.

An example of an assessment sheet for recording physical ability to carry out a specific gardening task (reprinted from McChesney, 1994).

Other methods of assessment are also used, for example, in-depth appraisal interviews, video recording and photography in addition to general, informal appraisals. These records not only help project organisers to monitor and record their clients' progress, they also help the clients themselves see the growth in their skills and help to raise self-confidence. Video recording can be a particularly useful format as it is accessible and easily interpreted.

It is important that consent is obtained prior to taking photographs or making video recordings and that images of clients are not used elsewhere, for example in publicity material or magazine articles, without permission. Written consent protects both the project organiser and the client.

An initial assessment can be carried out soon after a client has joined the project and is reasonably comfortable with attending. This will determine the general areas of ability and will be a starting point for planning further training or activities. It will also uncover any specific difficulties that the client may have in relation to the project activities. The assessment will

---

[3] Thrive publishes a range of information and briefing sheets on a wide variety of subjects related to STH projects, for example, 'Gardens and gardening for people with dementia', 'Working with volunteers', and 'Planning gardens for children with special needs'. For details see the Thrive website publications page: www.thrive.org.uk/page06.html

also find out their motives for attending the project and their ambitions and goals for the future. It will help the client choose suitable activities and may allow them to suggest new ones that are of particular interest to them.

The initial assessment can be combined with an induction to the project showing the client all of the features and facilities. A checklist of items for the induction may prove useful. Although some project organisers carry out the initial assessment in an informal manner by way of a 'chat', a written record of the assessment helps the organiser to plan activities and is necessary when progress and goals are reviewed. This should be carried out regularly and at predetermined times rather than on an ad hoc or casual basis. The length of time between reviews will vary according to the type of assessment. For example, some project staff carry out assessments of specific tasks at every client visit or on a weekly basis; appraisal interviews and more detailed reviews can be carried out every three or six months.

Such assessments contribute to measures of progress generally referred to as 'soft outcomes'. These are not quantifiable in an absolute sense but are measures of personal achievement. They may be based on subjective assessments, but may also include specific measures, or indicators, of achievement or competence collected by the methods described above. Soft outcomes also include factors such as motivation, personal and social skills, and practical skills, for example, horticultural knowledge and skills that can be evaluated by observing specific tasks. Studies of soft outcomes identify four 'core' areas:

* key work skills
* attitudinal skills
* personal skills
* practical skills.

Additional outcome areas can be identified for the target client group and indicators developed for that particular outcome. Each outcome, therefore, will be associated with a group of indicators. The outcomes and indicators chosen will depend on the client group and the project activities. A useful publication on soft outcomes and 'distance travelled' is available form the Institute for Employment Studies[4].

---

[4] Dewson, S., Eccles, J., Tackey, N.D. and Jackson, A. (2001) *Guide to measuring soft outcomes and distance travelled*, Brighton: Institute for Employment Studies. Available at: www.employment-studies.co.uk/pubs/report.php?id=soft

See also Lloyd, R. and O'Sullivan, F. (2002) *Measuring soft outcomes and distance travelled – A practical guide*, available from the publications page of the website of the European Social Fund: www.esf.gov.uk/evaluation/publications.asp

Distance travelled in this case refers to the progress made towards employment (or being employable). The authors comment that:

> Indicators (or measurements) of soft outcomes can be used as tools for measuring distance travelled towards labour market participation. (Dewson et al, 2001, p 3)

However, distance travelled need not refer just to employment; it can be used as a measure of progress towards any chosen goal. Soft outcomes can also be intermediate steps on the progression to 'hard outcomes', that is, measurable and quantifiable factors such as employment or qualifications. Although these may be measures of individual achievements, they can also be functions of the project as a whole, for example, the number of clients using a project, the number finding paid employment or the number of clients gaining a particular qualification. The collection of such information may be useful when demonstrating a project's ability to deliver services, but there may be few hard outcomes to report. The process of assessment and monitoring of soft outcomes will show the success of the project and the impact of the efforts of the staff. These may not be apparent simply by looking at hard outcome statistics.

An appropriate assessment system will, therefore, help project staff to ensure that their clients receive the correct support to enable them to accomplish their desired goals and ambitions, either at the project or outside, and so fulfil their true potential. By identifying the needs of clients and responding to them, projects can be instrumental in promoting social inclusion. Assessment also enables clients to see their own development and progress and it demonstrates the achievements of projects in respect of their clients.

Finding and keeping employment

It is frequently considered that finding employment is the aim of many clients; however, only around 30% of respondents in the Growing Together study reported that they were using the project as a means of finding paid work. Most of the project organisers reported that fewer than 10% of clients actually found employment. They also reported that a substantial proportion of those finding work did not remain employed. There may be many reasons for this, for example, the job may not have been suitable or the client may not have been fully prepared for work. It is also possible that prejudice still exists against clients with physical or mental disabilities or problems. The 1995 Disability Discrimination Act, however, makes it illegal for employers (those with 15 or more employees) to discriminate against a disabled employee or job applicant by treating them less favourably than other employees or applicants on the grounds of their disability. It also obliges employers to make 'reasonable adjustments' or modifications for disabled employees. If disabled employees consider that they have been victims of discrimination, they can take their case to an industrial tribunal under the terms of the Act.

Further information on the Disability Discrimination Act is available from the government's disability rights website: www.disability.gov.uk/dda/. A code of practice, 'Elimination of discrimination in the field of employment against disabled persons or persons who have had a disability' can be downloaded from the site.
Additional advice can be obtained from the Disability Rights Commission: www.drc-gb.org/

Facilitating a client's move into employment has to be well managed to ensure success. Loss of employment can lead to a loss of self-confidence, self-esteem and status that may have taken considerable effort on both the part of the project and client to achieve. Projects that had been set up with the specific aim of providing training for employment were generally successful in that aim. However, substantial resources were often necessary to support the clients. For example, some projects were able to arrange an initial series of supported placements at work that gave the prospective employee a chance to try out the environment and the work. Attendance was gradually increased until the target level of employment was reached. Support workers accompanied clients for up to a year and took away the feelings of panic – of being thrown in at the 'deep end'. Employers were supportive of such arrangements that generally worked well. However, difficulties were occasionally encountered with trainees who progressed particularly slowly and became reliant on the project and experienced difficulties in adapting to the workplace. One project organiser described the case of a client who was found a place in employment but deliberately behaved badly in order to attempt to return to the training project. The 'Access to Work' scheme, administered by Jobcentre Plus, is designed to help disabled people in the workplace. It provides advice and information to employees and employers and also pays a grant towards any extra employment costs that arise as a result of an employee's disability (further information is available from Jobcentre Plus, either through a local office or the website: www.jobcentreplus.gov.uk).

Contacting potential employers

Some project organisers have simply identified potential employers and approached them directly. Others have become involved with initiatives teaching employers about disabilities and the 1995 Disability Discrimination Act and have developed a relationship that way. Another approach has been through involvement with company team-building exercises. Large companies have used a number of projects for such activities. They provide the opportunity for a team of employees to work on a specific task on a project, such as clearing derelict land. Some of those engaged in the team-building strategies have continued to work on projects as volunteers in their spare time. Where ideas exist for tasks that could be used for team building, these can be written up as proposals and sent to companies and businesses likely to respond. These have included banks, credit card companies and large stores. Participating in local networks can prove valuable in obtaining information about such companies and the Community Service Volunteers (CSV) can offer help in making contact with organisations and companies looking for 'team tasks' or projects to support (www.csv.org.uk/). Local 'green' and environmental partnerships are also a useful forum for contacting potential employers.

Projects as a source of employment

Projects can provide employment in a number of different ways. Clients often become volunteers and helpers at projects as their condition improves and their confidence increases. They may progress to paid employment as therapists or project organisers. In those positions they have a specialised knowledge of the benefits and limitations of the project and a unique insight into the difficulties and challenges facing clients. Sometimes new activities have been started at projects and these have enabled clients to be taken on as paid employees, for example, recycling and composting schemes or projects have set up social firms (see page 36) and cooperatives to follow various commercial ventures.

Suitability for employment

Not all clients will be suitable for employment, and not all employment will be suitable for clients. The workplace may have contributed to the problems experienced by many of those with mental ill health and the prospect of returning to work may be a daunting one. However, some project organisers reported that on occasions they felt pressured into progressing clients into employment by various schemes and initiatives that funded 'training' or 'preparation for work'. Although these were a welcome source of income, they did not necessarily take account of clients' needs. For example, the schemes operated over a fixed period of time and the assumption was that the client would be ready for work at the end of the training. The success of such initiatives was often measured by rates of employment rather than by the clients' health or well-being. The desire to achieve 'successful' outcomes and statistics should not have a detrimental effect on the clients. Projects, however, often found ways of extending a client's stay at the project by finding additional funding so that someone was not pushed into work when they were not ready for it.

Pay and expenses

Some of the projects were able to pay their clients' expenses or attendance allowance, others (cooperatives) divided the surplus monies raised from commercial ventures among the project participants. Pay was always highly regarded even when the actual amounts of money were low and contributed to the clients' perception of their status as a 'worker'.

Some projects are engaged in production for an established marketplace, for example, those operating nurseries, while others engage in some form of commercial activity to a lesser extent. Income derived from this benefits the project and sometimes also the client. Around 26% of projects raise money through sales and contract work. However, the level of income generated by this is low – only around 10% of the total project budget. Many different commercial schemes have been operated by projects and there is room for expansion. It is important that the desire for income does not put undue pressure on the clients as work carried out in the open marketplace has to be of a comparable standard to the competition.

Welfare benefits and pay

Project staff should understand the welfare benefits system in particular as the receipt of pay and expenses may adversely affect their clients' entitlement to a range of benefits. Income-related benefits, such as Housing Benefit, may be affected if earnings exceed the 'earnings disregard' limit, currently £20 a week for the long-term sick and disabled. Similarly, Incapacity Benefit and Severe Disablement Allowance will be affected if earnings exceed the 'Permitted Work' limit, formerly known as the 'therapeutic earnings limit' (the working time allowed is 16 hours per week for 26 weeks).

The state benefits system is complex. The Department for Work and Pensions (DWP) publishes a series of guides to the system, including a 'Concise guide to pensions, and tax credits', which lists all of the other guides and publications. Some of these are particularly detailed, such as the 'Guide to Housing Benefit and Council Tax Benefit', which is 144 pages long.

DWP guides to state benefits are available on the Internet from the 'resource centre's website: www.dwp.gov.uk/resourcecentre/index.asp and information can be obtained from Jobcentre Plus and council offices, and from the local Citizens' Advice Bureau. The Child Poverty Action Group also publishes a series of detailed guides to various benefits, which can be downloaded from their website: www.cpag.org.uk/

The 'Benefit Enquiry Line for People with Disabilities' is a confidential telephone advice and information service that deals with welfare benefit queries from disabled people, their carers and representatives.
Telephone: 0800 882200
Textphone: 0800 243355

'Therapeutic wages'

Some project organisers have recently expressed concern regarding payments of expenses and allowances to clients because of issues regarding the National Minimum Wage (NMW). If any payment is made to clients, should that be in line with the NMW? The NMW is payable to all those whose *legal* status is that of a 'worker', that is, they have a contract or agreement with their employer, they have an obligation to carry out work to a set level of productivity or standard and they are rewarded for the work actually done:

> ... if a person is paid more than expenses and is obliged
> to perform an activity in accordance with the employer's
> instructions, the individual is likely to be entitled to the
> minimum wage. (DTI guidance document[5])

Minimum wage legislation also applies to members of a cooperative if they are employees of that cooperative and carry out work under a contract and are paid specifically for it. Few, if any, clients are under an obligation to be productive at garden projects and may choose to leave early or arrive late if they wish. Apart from those participating in social firms, it is doubtful if any would come under the legal definition of 'worker'. There is no reason, therefore, why projects should not pay clients' expenses and attendance allowances if they are able. This in itself will not bring them under minimum wage legislation.

Summary

Identify the aims and goals of clients and provide suitable activities.

Assess progress, monitor outcomes and review goals regularly and at pre-arranged times.

Develop a means of progression within the project.

Ensure that clients who find employment receive adequate support.

Establish rapport with potential employers.

If starting out to provide training for employment, ensure that you have the necessary resources.

If paying expenses or 'therapeutic wages', understand the impact such payments will have on clients' entitlement to welfare benefits.

---

5   A guidance document, *The Minimum Wage and therapeutic work* (updated May 2003) is available from the Department of Trade and Industry (DTI) and can be downloaded from the Internet: www.dti.gov.uk/er/nmw/nmwther.pdf

3 Managing the project

Managing the project

Evidence of quality

Quality Assurance (QA) systems are designed to improve an organisation's performance by examining its activities in a systematic manner in specific key areas, for example, managing staff and resources, financial management, and training and development. By focusing on what an organisation does, what it does well and by identifying areas for improvement, the quality of service delivery to the client can be improved. The ability of staff to deliver those services can also be improved and this contributes to greater client and staff satisfaction.

Although there is no statutory requirement for the use of any QA system for STH, the area is currently undergoing a period of self-assessment and increasing professionalism. Referring agencies are obliged to procure high quality services for their clients from providers who are able to demonstrate that quality. Equally, practitioners want to do a good job and be recognised for that. Therefore, it is necessary to have in place a system that monitors and improves the quality of services and management.

A new QA system has been developed by Thrive specifically for horticulture projects and will be launched in 2005. It is entitled *Cultivating Quality* and has been adapted from the Practical Quality Assurance System for Small Organisations (PQASSO) system used by small organisations and charities. The original system was developed by Charities Evaluation Services (CES) and its adaptation was carried out with the cooperation and approval of CES (for more details about PQASSO see the CES website: www.ces-vol.org.uk/).

Cultivating Quality is a self-assessment system in which evidence of quality is collected and examined against a series of criteria in the key areas of the project. For example, one criterion is the competence of staff in the area of horticulture relevant to the activities they deliver. Evidence of competence can be formal qualifications, awards, Continuing Professional Development records, a portfolio of work or other documentation. The project has the freedom of choice in terms of the type of evidence used. Such assessment can help a project improve its management, governance and service delivery activities against a set of standards and to review them periodically.

While Cultivating Quality and other QA systems allow managers to examine their projects in a systematic way, this guide aims to highlight those areas of project practice that are important and that have an impact on the quality of service and delivery. Hence, ideas from this guide will help to develop and strengthen aspects of STH services as set out in Cultivating Quality or other QA systems.

Summary

Using a quality assurance system can help to improve the management of a project and the service it offers.

Aims and objectives

Although the implicit aim of most (if not all) projects is to promote health and well-being for their clients, some have specific aims, for example, finding or providing employment or teaching organic gardening techniques. It is useful to have a clear view of these objectives and to test the performance of projects with these in mind, also, to review those aims and objectives periodically and to modify them if required. For example, if the project has been set up to help clients find employment, does it fulfil that role? If clients do not find employment it does not necessarily mean that the project has failed – especially if the clients' well-being has improved. The following questions can be asked:

* What are the aims and objectives of the project?
* Are they realistic or achievable?
* What measure and indicators are in place?
* Is the project fulfilling the aims and objectives?
* If not, why not?
* Should the aims be changed or should the activities be altered?

Most projects produce leaflets or brochures describing their activities and include some details of their aims and objectives. However, these can sometimes be vague and generalised. A short 'mission statement' can be effective. Although to some the idea of a 'mission statement' may seem outdated or clichéd it is often an effective way of formally summarising and reinforcing key objectives.

Project identity

The identities of garden projects, to some extent like those of large corporations, are valuable assets, which can be used to promote projects and encourage and enthuse their clients. Our research has shown that clients identify strongly with their particular projects, and being part of a project can reinforce feelings of belonging and loyalty:

"I think I felt very accepted by everybody, and the feeling when I've, sort of, not been well enough even to get myself here, eventually coming back and everybody being so welcoming, and being able to just join in with whatever was happening, erm, whether it was the gardening, or the woodwork, or the blacksmithing, it's just, it's so easy to fall back into. You know, the garden side seems [...] it keeps going, but it's, there's still a place for you in it." (client with mental health problems)

The aims and objectives of a project can be put succinctly in the advertising leaflet.

Looking for something a bit different?

The Green Health Partnership provides opportunities for people living with mental health problems to become involved in practical conservation and horticultural activities.

We are based at The Gardens in Shipley Country Park and can give you the chance to join in a wide range of practical conservation activities ranging from tree planting and nursery work to footpath construction and environmental art.

Our main objectives are to provide a supportive environment in which you can develop practical and personal skills, work towards qualifications and be part of a friendly team working to improve the environment. Some of the benefits you may get from volunteering include improving your mental & physical health, building confidence and self-esteem.

©Bill Sillburn

A strong identity and an interesting name can help to promote a project.

Summary

Set clear aims and objectives for the project.

Consider whether a 'mission statement' may be useful.

Examine whether the project is meeting its aims and objectives.

Use your identity to promote the work of the project and its clients.

Sustainable practices and organic gardening

Many projects will use organic methods of gardening, but only a small number may be registered as organic. In the Growing Together study only one or two projects used herbicides or pesticides, and only because they were involved in certain commercial horticultural activities and considered that their use was unavoidable in those circumstances. They preferred to use 'sustainable' gardening methods where possible. In addition to environmental concerns over herbicides and pesticides, issues of health and safety and supervision are also critical factors. Projects should consider these issues carefully before opting to use chemical agents. Organic gardening techniques and sustainable environmental practices are useful to garden projects for a number of reasons:

* Many projects consider organic and environmentally sustainable practices as a 'good thing'. Being involved with them allows the clients to be part of that 'good thing'. There is a sense of contributing to the overall well-being of society and that in turn may improve well-being and self-esteem.
* An increased level of care, attention and knowledge is required for organic production. This can provide a useful opportunity for the development of new skills. It has also proved to be an opportunity for some projects to develop new courses for teaching organic gardening methods. These can be accredited by local colleges or set up in partnership with them. If the project organisers are not acquainted with organic methods it enables them to learn something new in partnership with their clients.
* Confidence in the products – some clients who have had drug or alcohol problems or have been on long-term medication have become wary of all chemicals. One client who attended a project for unemployed people and those on a low income described all supermarket products as 'a lie' because they looked attractive but he did not know (and did not trust) what pesticides or fertilisers had been used in their cultivation. Thus, for him, the consumption of organic produce was a way of ridding himself of the problems that chemicals had caused him.
* Organically produced fruit and vegetables have a 'unique selling point' and attract a high premium in shops and supermarkets. Some consumers have now become mistrustful of the 'organic' status of produce in supermarkets because of the many different standards in operation. Thus, gardening projects that produce and sell organic produce to the public are often highly valued in local communities. Sales of organic

produce also help to promote projects and their work as they help to strengthen links with local communities.

- Environmental issues are an important topic of public interest and political debate. Some projects invite guest speakers to talk about specific topics such as sustainable and organic gardening methods. These events can trigger debate among clients and project staff about topical and political issues. This may also lead to new associations with other social or environmental networks either local or national, for example, the Black Environment Network (BEN).

- Sustainable environmental practices can provide opportunities for the creation of new activities and initiatives. There are many examples of such schemes, for example, community composting schemes, cardboard recycling schemes, building of composting toilets, and construction and erection of wind generators and solar panels.

- Organic methods and sustainable practices at projects may attract volunteers and staff. Many of those who work or volunteer on garden projects have been encouraged to help out or offer their services because of a shared interest in organic gardening and the environment.

Sustainable environmental practices are an integral part of many STH projects and may enhance the feeling of well-being.

Summary

Sustainable environmental practices enable clients to identify with a 'good thing'.

They may help to attract volunteers and visitors to the project.

They can form the basis of many different activities.

They generate interest and discussion.

Financial management

The need to increase or find new sources of funding is a constant pressure for most garden projects. Competition for resources is often fierce and financial security appears to be restricted only to those projects with large parent organisations. Thus, fundraising skills are critical in respect of project organisers' experience, and fundraising activities often take up a significant portion of their time. However, it is often easier to find money to start a new project than to find the resources to meet running costs. Funding bodies are often more keen to fund the first two or three years of a project's life than to provide subsequent funds (although there have been schemes that have been aimed at meeting the running costs of various types of projects for disabled and vulnerable people). Similarly, it is often easier to find funds for a new venture within a project, such as constructing a new garden feature or a building than to meet core costs such as the project organiser's salary. The survey of projects yielded some interesting, and potentially useful information regarding project costs and financial management.

Projects obtain their funding from a wide variety of different sources and most rely on multiple sources of funding, although 38% rely on a single source. Around 10% make a charge directly to their clients while more than half (54%) receive fees for clients from local authorities and health trusts. These can be paid on a per capita basis for named individuals but at times a 'block' fee is paid to the projects to provide a service for a set number of client placements. The average fee charged on behalf of a client per session is £27 and 86% of projects charge between £10 and £60. However, the average cost of a client session is calculated to be £54 – the same as the cost of a session at a local authority or NHS day centre – and twice as much as the average client fee. This suggests that projects are undercharging for their services and, as a result, are forced to find additional funding through grants, sales and so on. Project organisers report that local authorities, health trusts and other organisations that use their services – for example, schools – are often unwilling to pay increased charges. Some would sooner not use the service than pay more in fees. It is important to charge realistic client fees and to negotiate with agencies that use STH projects to ensure that realistic fees are agreed. A knowledge of the costs of other local services and a detailed breakdown of the costs of the project to show how client fees are derived will be useful in such discussions.

Around 10% of projects' total annual budget is from sales and commercial activity. The actual nature of this varies enormously – from casual sales of fruit and vegetables and arts and crafts to large-scale commercial plant production. However, few, if any, projects make an economic profit from their sales in order to be self-sufficient. These commercial ventures can be organised along the lines of social firms or cooperatives.

Social firms are businesses set up to create employment for disabled and vulnerable people. They aim to employ at least 25% of their paid workforce from this group and aim to achieve at least 50% of their income through sales or services and not be reliant on grants or subsidies. Social firms promote empowerment by paying standard market wages to all employees and involving them in decision making. Social firms are businesses that support individuals who are vulnerable rather than projects for vulnerable people that engage in some commercial activity.

However, some project organisers are reluctant to function as a social firm or to become heavily involved in commercial activity on the grounds that this may place too great a pressure on clients. Goods and services

Craft shops and other commercial enterprises not only generate income, they make the project more visible and strengthen links with the local community.

For more information about social firms see www.socialfirms.co.uk/or the Social Enterprise Unit of the Department of Trade and Industry: www.dti.gov.uk/socialenterprise/

offered on the open market need to be of sufficiently high quality to make them attractive. If there are any inconsistencies in quality, and subsequent complaints, this may be particularly distressing for some clients. Therefore, appropriate consultation with the client group is essential before projects engage in commercial activities. It is possible that clients with mental health problems, for example, may have developed problems as a result of work and thus may be less suited to a commercial environment. Others, who may have never been employed and are seeking to engage with the labour market in some way, would perhaps benefit from participation in commercial production.

From a financial point of view, a garden project is little different from a small business (in most cases). It requires a steady inflow of funds in order to pay its costs (running costs and wages). However, the income may be fixed because of standard fees or supporting payments and may also be dependent on grants and donations and so be uncertain. The cash flow may be disrupted by delays in payments, or by special conditions attached to grants, for example, grants may be paid in arrears for items that have already been purchased and paid for. It may also have a seasonal dimension, for example, it may rely on the sale of plants or produce. For this reason many projects experience difficulties with cash flow. It is an often repeated maxim that more businesses fail because of a lack of cash than as a result of a lack of profit. The cash flow needs to be kept under close scrutiny by preparation of forecasts and managed where possible. In order to do this, proper financial records need to be kept and some training is helpful. Many colleges run book-keeping and accounting courses for small businesses and these will be both interesting and useful to project staff and also to some volunteers and clients. Additionally, accounts packages are available for home computers; many of these, such as Quicken, are inexpensive and easy to use. Getting to grips with such a piece of software can present an interesting challenge to some clients and a boost in self-confidence and self-esteem.

Summary

Keep a proper financial record.

Collate and understand annual running cost statistics, including unit costs per client session.

Charge a realistic client fee – as close as possible to the actual costs.

Negotiate with social services and health trusts for adequate payments.

Be aware of the requirements and criteria of funding agencies and explore new sources of funding.

Produce a business plan and financial flow chart for new ventures and have them to hand if new funding opportunities arise unexpectedly.

If you are starting a new project estimate running costs beyond the initial start-up funding.

If engaging in commercial ventures do not do this at the expense of the clients.

Staffing needs

Staffing needs at projects vary according to project size, facilities offered, number of clients and the nature of the client group. For example, more staff may be required for people with learning difficulties than for other groups as they often need a greater level of supervision or help – some may require assistance on a one-to-one basis for a large proportion of their sessions at the project. However, this will depend on the degree of disability, numbers and so on.

A realistic assessment of project staffing needs is required, together with a plan to achieve the numbers required – whether using paid staff or volunteers. Working on an STH project requires a variety of skills and it may take a long time to find a suitable person to fill a vacancy.

A realistic expectation of staff is also necessary. Many project founders have worked long hours in order to realise their ambitions or visions for their projects. It is entirely reasonable of them to expect their staff to have a commitment to the project; however, they should not expect staff to work routinely beyond their contracted hours or terms. Project managers should also take an interest in the career development and aspirations of their staff. Regular appraisal interviews help to assess training and development needs and enable staff to progress within the project.

Some project organisers take on so much work that the project can become entirely dependent on them and their contribution. Should they decide to leave the project, its future may then be uncertain. Delegation of tasks and responsibilities at an early stage in the project's life is therefore a good idea. Contingency plans for coping in the event of staff illness or absence are also necessary.

Staff training and qualifications

Many diverse qualities and skills are required to run a successful project including practical, organisational and social skills. Project organisers come from many different backgrounds including horticulture, occupational therapy, teaching and nursing. Many have gained on-the-job experience or are self-taught. However, there are a number of different training courses available to help those who are intending to, or already run or work on gardening projects.

Clearly, horticultural knowledge is essential and around 40% of staff working on projects have qualifications in horticulture and many of the others have acquired on-the-job training and skills. Although there is no absolute requirement for STH project staff to have horticultural qualifications, it would be advantageous for a number of reasons. Attending a formal programme of learning helps to fill any gaps in knowledge; it provides a useful record of achievement when moving to another project or employer; and it helps to raise professional standards in this important area.

There are a number of different training and qualification options available, from the Royal Horticultural Society (RHS) General Certificate in Horticulture through to HND, degree or higher degree. While most people studying at degree level will be taking full-time courses, many of the other qualifications can be obtained through part-time, evening or distance learning. For example, many further education colleges offer BTEC National Certificate courses in horticulture. The BTEC can be taken as a one-year, full-time course or two years studying one day per week. The more advanced National Diploma requires two years of study. The RHS General Certificate can be obtained by studying at evening classes and also by distance learning.

Only around 10% of garden projects employ staff with a qualification in 'therapeutic horticulture'. Again, while there is no absolute need for formal qualifications in the subject, attainment of these by STH staff would serve to increase the professional identity of projects and their staff. Professional Development Certificate and Diploma courses in therapeutic horticulture are offered by Coventry University in conjunction with Thrive. These are provided in a 'flexible learning format' over a period of one year (part-time) so that students with work and other commitments can also participate (further details are available from Thrive).

Certificate and Diploma courses provide training in the latest approaches and techniques in STH and offer students an opportunity for contact with others in the profession. Basic training in STH can be obtained by attending a relevant 'short course', such as one of those described below.

Thrive and the BTCV provide many short training courses that may be useful for project staff and volunteers.

Short courses in STH and related subjects

Many training providers and institutions run short (one-day and weekend) courses that will be relevant for those working in the field of STH. For example:

* Thrive runs a variety of courses including training in horticultural skills, how to develop and run horticultural therapy programmes, recruiting volunteers, working with people with special needs (for details see the Thrive website training page: www.thrive.org.uk/page07.html).
* The British Trust for Conservation Volunteers (BTCV) offers a variety of short courses (one-day and weekend) that are useful to garden project workers. These include leadership skills, project management and finance, conservation skills, risk assessment, publicity and fundraising and many more (for details contact BTCV or download their training brochure from www.btcv.org). Some of these are organised in partnership with other institutions and organisations such as Thrive. The BTCV also runs a wide-ranging programme of courses on behalf of the Environmental Trainers Network (see www.btcv.org/etn/). This programme includes courses on preparing effective funding applications, consultation techniques, making partnerships and working with local communities.

Counselling

Both formal and informal counselling for vulnerable clients is an integral part of project activity. Some projects employ qualified counsellors and provide formal sessions for their clients rather than relying on the informality of a 'garden chat'. Others encourage their staff to undergo basic training in counselling and working with people with mental health problems and learning difficulties. There are a number of organisations and colleges that provide training in these skills.

For further information on counselling courses contact the British Association for Counselling and Psychotherapy at www.bacp.co.uk/ or local colleges.

Other useful training

There are a number of other courses and training opportunities that could be useful for project staff and volunteers, for example, information technology, including word processing, use of spreadsheets and finance packages. Individual IT skills vary enormously across projects. An improvement in IT skills more generally could be useful in a number of different ways, for example, in the preparation of teaching material, handouts and presentations, websites and publicity material.

Practical courses on rural and land-based skills and crafts are also available (see, for example, the BTCV training brochure) and these can lead to the introduction of new activities for clients.

Summary

Assess staffing needs and provisions.

Make an audit of the qualifications and training needs of staff and volunteers.

For those members of staff who do not have any formal qualifications in horticulture, consider offering opportunities for new qualifications, such as a RHS General Certificate. Contact your local college for details of courses, or contact the RHS for details of distance learning providers.

Consider a Certificate or Diploma in therapeutic horticulture.

Have a look at the short training courses, for example, those offered by Thrive and BTCV.

Volunteers

Many projects recruit unpaid volunteers to help with project maintenance or to work alongside clients, or both. However, some projects have a specific policy of only using paid staff as they consider that the difficulties involved in the recruitment, vetting and training of people to work alongside vulnerable clients on a voluntary or casual basis outweigh any benefits. The decision whether or not to use volunteers should form part of the management strategy of the project and the recruitment of volunteers should be viewed in a similar manner to the recruitment of staff if they are to work alongside clients, that is, appropriate checks should be carried out.

The needs of volunteers, and the blurred boundary that may exist between clients and volunteers, has already been mentioned. Some of those who join projects as 'volunteers' do so simply because they have time on their hands and view STH projects as a worthy cause. Others, however, may have needs similar to those of the clients and may require a similar level of support.

It is therefore necessary to identify the needs and motives of potential volunteers in addition to their skills and experience and to plan how they will be used at the project and how support can be provided, or, indeed, if it is possible to provide the necessary support. Volunteers bring a variety of skills and experience to projects including gardening skills, engineering and construction, teaching, healthcare and many others. Projects offer them the opportunity to use those skills, particularly when a change in circumstances such as retirement or a move to a house without a garden has resulted in them being unable to practice those skills. A plan for the personal development of volunteers and progress at the project will help to maintain their interest in the long term. This should include an assessment of training needs, as for paid staff.

In many cases, volunteers arrive at projects as clients and move on to work there as unpaid helpers. Some have subsequently progressed to paid employment at the projects, for example, as therapists, organisers and managers. The experience and skills that they have acquired at the project have enabled them to make that transition. It is valuable for clients to be able to see that such a pathway for progression is possible.

Many garden tasks are carried out by unpaid volunteers, some of whom also have support needs.

Recruitment of volunteers

Some projects experience difficulties in recruiting volunteers while some of the larger ones have waiting lists. Volunteers are attracted to projects for many reasons, for example, an association with the particular client group or an affinity to the aims of the project. Others may have an interest in the type of gardening or the history of the garden, or an interest in specific activities at the project. It is useful therefore to publicise the activities and aims of the project as widely as possible and to encourage the local community to engage with the project (see Chapter 4). Open days have been successful in recruiting volunteers. Other approaches have included recruitment campaigns using advertising in local newspapers, leaflets and posters, websites and contact with voluntary groups and charities. Local volunteer bureaus have also proved useful.

It is essential when recruiting volunteers that projects recognise and implement a number of safeguards in order to ensure safe and effective working practices. These include:

- Providing comprehensive information for volunteers and clients about successful working relationships, issues such as confidentiality, respect for others and health and safety and complaints procedures (some of these will be specific project policies).

- Volunteers who will be working alongside certain client groups (particularly on a one-to-one basis) such as those with learning difficulties or mental health problems, ideally should have some experience of working with these groups.
- Projects should consider implementing a Criminal Records Bureau (CRB) check for volunteers in order to ascertain whether volunteers have any previous convictions that may mean they should not work with vulnerable groups, particularly where children are involved.
- Issues relating to risk management and health and safety procedures should apply equally to project staff, clients and volunteers/helpers.

Summary

Understand the wishes of volunteers (and clients) and be sensitive to terminology adopted.

Implement formal referral procedures by developing links with health and social care agencies.

Have protocols in place for the safe and effective recruitment of volunteers and for the protection of clients.

Ensure volunteers, project staff and clients are familiar with project policies (on confidentiality and risk assessment).

Managing risk

Health and safety legislation (see the Management of Health and Safety at Work Regulations, 1999) requires employers to assess the risks to their employees as a result of the activities they undertake, and also the risks to others, including visitors and customers. In other words, project organisers have a duty of care to assess and implement health and safety measures not only in respect of clients but also other project workers, volunteers and members of the public who visit the project site.

In our research study we found little evidence of accidents or reports of physical injury to clients or staff. This may reflect the inherently safe nature of gardening and the diligence of project organisers. However, since around 400,000 accidents a year occur in the garden (around 20% of domestic accidents) of which approximately 18% are considered 'serious' or 'very serious', the issue of risk needs to be considered. Risk assessment is simply a logical way of asking questions about the activities and features on a project site. One approach is to use a 'five-point method' like that described in Appendix D.

There are three main areas of risk that relate to a STH project:

- site-specific risks that are related to specific areas or features of the garden project, for example, a set of steps or ramps. These will pose a different level of risk to different individuals on the project;

- risks to clients, volunteers, staff and visitors from the project activities, tools and machinery. These can be considered as independent processes;
- risks to clients, volunteers and staff from other clients, volunteers and staff.

A risk assessment could first consider site-specific risks. Surprisingly, almost half of garden accidents are caused by falls on hard surfaces, steps or lawns and only a small proportion (around 2%) are caused by tools and machinery.

Risks from project activities can then be examined. Clients with physical disabilities or mental health problems may be at greater risk of accident or injury than those without such disabilities or problems and the degree of risk will vary from client to client according to the level of disability. It will also change with time as the client's condition improves or deteriorates. Some projects, therefore, produce a personal risk assessment for each client, considering the risk from each of the activities performed by them and the measures taken to minimise those risks, for example, use of a specific garden tool such as a spade or rake; or tasks such as planting or weeding. Each client can then be assessed against a range of specific tasks to produce a personal risk assessment and appropriate training in the use of tools and safety precautions can be given. Such an assessment should take into account the client's abilities, stamina, medication and any other relevant factors.

Other projects take a more general view of the risks associated with project activities and assess a client's ability to work on the project as a whole, while identifying any issues that pose a specific risk to an individual, for example, the use of a mower or power tools. Training needs can be identified for each activity or tool as required. Whatever the assessment method used, a written or computer record enables the client's progress and training to be monitored.

Risks from clients, staff and volunteers

While risks from garden activities and features are fairly straightforward to assess, those arising from people may be far more problematic. Clients are drawn from a vulnerable population and may include people with mental health problems, drug and alcohol problems, offending backgrounds and victims of abuse. Individual clients may have a number of these problems and it is conceivable for ex-offenders to be working alongside victims of crime or abuse. It is important to note here that clients are usually referred to projects by social services or Community Mental Health Teams (CMHTs) and their history is known to those agencies. Their suitability for the project can be assessed by a day visit to the project and discussions with the case worker or social worker. It is usual for prospective clients to make their initial visits to a project with their case workers. However, some project organisers have spoken of difficulties in obtaining information from referring agencies. In one specific incident, information about the deterioration of a patient's condition was not passed on to a project organiser who subsequently suffered a serious assault at the hands of that patient leading to a considerable time off work. It is essential, therefore, to ensure that good lines of communication are open with those agencies and individuals involved in the care and referral of clients so that such incidents are avoided and the likelihood of unsuitable placements is minimised. Projects should not be afraid to turn away clients that they suspect may be unsuitable or disruptive.

Some clients self-refer to projects. Project workers are therefore dependent, to a large extent, on the client to provide his or her medical or social history. Unfortunately, some projects do not enquire too closely about such clients' backgrounds as they consider that to do so would be intrusive. Instead, they opt to 'keep a careful eye' on newcomers and supervise their activities closely, especially when their work involves contact with other, vulnerable people. However, such an ad hoc arrangement could lead to problems and it would be beneficial if all projects were fully informed of their clients' backgrounds. Many projects choose only to accept clients from referring agencies such as social services. In that way clients' medical histories are known and any likely problems can be anticipated. A clear policy on admission of clients is necessary.

The role of volunteers at projects has already been discussed. Many volunteers are also vulnerable and are seeking an opportunity to engage in a worthwhile activity and to develop structure in their lives. Some have had alcohol and drug problems and some have had criminal convictions for these and other offences. Although it is essential to provide a safe environment for all clients and to ensure that they are not put at risk from other clients, volunteers or staff, the possession of a criminal record should not be a barrier to either employment or acceptance as a volunteer. However, projects need to look carefully at those whose record suggests that they could pose a risk to vulnerable clients.

The law (through the 1997 Police Act) now allows potential employers to gain access to the criminal records of potential employees and volunteers through the CRB by means of a process of 'disclosures'. A 'Standard Disclosure' gives details of a person's convictions, including those classified as spent under the 1974 Rehabilitation of Offenders Act, and any warnings, cautions or reprimands which are held on the police national computer. An 'Enhanced Disclosure' includes any additional information held by local police forces in their records (for further information see Appendix E).

All projects should consider whether they should (or need to) use the CRB disclosure system.

Training

The BTCV provides training courses for risk assessment in a conservation environment and also relevant first aid courses (for details see the BTCV training brochure, which is available on the Trust's website: www.btcv.org/).

First aid

Part of the management of risk is to provide appropriate first aid equipment and employ people with the right training. This is a requirement of the 1981 Health and Safety (First-Aid) Regulations, which apply to all workplaces including those with five or fewer employees and also the self-employed. Government agencies provide a range of information about health and safety, which is available on the Internet. The website of the Health and Safety Executive (HSE) provides useful information on first aid (www.hse.gov.uk/firstaid/) including the leaflet 'First aid at work' (www.hse.gov.uk/pubns/indg214.pdf), which contains a checklist of items to consider when assessing first aid requirements. The HSE also publishes a guide to the regulations[6].

Recording and reporting accidents

In addition to the assessment of risk, and its management, a process for dealing with incidents and accidents and recording these details is necessary. A formal process helps staff and volunteers to make consistent and logical decisions. Since December 2003 methods of recording accidents must comply with the 1988 Data Protection Act, insomuch that anyone recording an accident must not be able to read the previous entries. The HSE publishes an 'Accident Book' (BI 510), which contains tear-off reporting forms that can be stored securely once they have been completed. The publication also contains useful information about accident reporting.

Certain serious accidents (and potentially dangerous incidents) need to be reported to the HSE under the Reporting of Injuries, Diseases and Dangerous Occurrences (RIDDOR). These include death, major injury and injury that necessitates more than three days off work. Further information is available from the HSE (see www.riddor.gov.uk/).

---

6   HSE (Health and Safety Executive) (1997) *First aid at work. The 1981 Health and Safety (First-Aid) Regulations,* Approved Code of Practice and Guidance, L74, London: HSE Books, ISBN 0 7176 1050 0.

Health and safety policy document

There are, therefore, a number of issues associated with health and safety that need to be considered and of which staff and volunteers need to be aware. All of these issues can be grouped together under a health and safety policy for the project.

The HSE publishes a booklet, 'Stating your business', directed at small businesses (but which is also relevant to STH projects) in order to help them prepare a health and safety policy document. This contains an outline policy statement that can be completed by the user and covers many aspects of health and safety policy including responsibilities, risks and accident reporting ('Stating your business' can be downloaded from the HSE website page for small businesses: www.hse.gov.uk/pubns/sfindex.htm). Additional procedures and processes specific to STH projects can be added to the document.

Summary

Carry out a risk assessment of the project site and activities.

Draw up a formal policy on acceptance of clients and recruitment of staff and volunteers.

Be familiar with legislation and regulations relevant to your project, for example, the need for CRB checks.

Prepare a health and safety policy document for your project.

4 Communication

Communication

There are a number of aspects to the communication strategies of STH projects. These include promotion, advertising and forming links with other agencies; communication between organisers, clients and volunteers; and information technology (IT); communication and training opportunities available to clients and volunteers at STH projects themselves.

Promotion and advertising

Promoting the work of STH projects is an effective way of attracting clients and volunteers as well as raising awareness of project work in local communities and organisations, such as health and social care agencies, academic institutions and funding bodies. Some projects engage in strategic promotional activities (while others do so on a more ad hoc basis depending on the availability of staff and resources) and have dedicated staff to organise promotional events, advertising and develop links locally and sometimes even nationally. While this type of work can be time consuming, many projects consider it important as it helps to attract clients and much needed funds.

There are a number of aspects to the communication strategies of STH projects; these include communication within the project and networking with different projects and organisations in addition to learning IT skills.

A number of projects create their own websites and produce regular updates in addition to newsletters and other material, for example, news about events such as seed swaps, flower shows and open days. Events such as these are effective ways of promoting the work of projects, of raising awareness in and among local public, business and charitable communities and making projects – and particularly clients – more visible. It is during open days and other public events that clients are encouraged to meet the public and to interact with people from local communities with whom they would not always have contact in their daily lives.

A flower show brings together many different projects and attracts visitors from the local community. It provides an obvious goal, that is, to win prizes. Receiving a prize enhances the feeling of satisfaction and the sense of achievement.

Many different events attract visitors, from open days to 'apple days'.

Some projects have produced videos featuring their work and products. One such project, for people recovering from mental illness, received a grant from the Community Fund to produce a video about their work, which will be distributed to GP surgeries. Most projects are able to produce some kind of information about their activities that can be distributed widely.

It is important to note here the importance of issues such as confidentiality and consent. In order to fully protect clients (as well as projects and their staff), projects should have clear confidentiality and consent policies or protocols in place. All information on clients should be stored safely but data that is used in promotional material, for example, photographs of projects on websites or in information leaflets, and which includes images of clients or volunteers, should only be used with the informed consent of those clients or volunteers.

Informed consent refers to procedures whereby those individuals have been fully informed of the need to use or include data for purposes other than record keeping (to which they should have open access) and the possible outcomes of giving permission to use that material. Any information on clients or volunteers that might be used for research purposes or by agencies outside the project should also only be used with the express permission of clients or volunteers and in accordance with projects' confidentiality policies.

Promotional materials can take many forms, from simple leaflets to websites and videos.

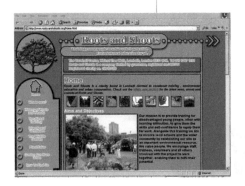

It may not always be possible for some clients to provide informed consent, especially where they have severe learning difficulties or impaired cognitive function. In these cases it is useful to refer to established procedures and protocols. For example, the British Psychological Society defines informed consent among vulnerable groups (such as those with learning difficulties) in the following way:

Where interventions are offered to those in no position to give valid consent, after consulting with experienced professional colleagues, establish who has legal authority to give consent and seek consent from that person or those persons. (British Psychological Society, article 36, p 3)

Communication within projects

Effective communication between project organisers, clients and volunteers is vital in order to maintain successful relationships within projects, ensure positive outcomes for clients and to maintain productivity. Some of the ways in which these objectives are achieved are in providing clients with the opportunity to give their opinions and feelings about the project, its work and the type and nature of services on offer. This can be done either through formal meetings, one-to-one discussions, appraisals or project meetings where organisers and clients get together on a regular basis. Most projects also keep records of meetings and of client progress (which are stored safely but are also readily accessible to clients).

Some projects also encourage clients and volunteers to produce their own material such as newsletters and information about the project from their own perspective. At one project for people with mental health problems the clients contributed to a 'storybook' about their experiences at the project (what they liked about it, the benefits of being part of the project and their future plans) and what they thought about the project organisers and how the project was run. As a result of this exercise new events were organised such as a regular gardening quiz between staff and client teams.

Many projects set up management or project committees, which enable clients to have their say and make important contributions to the way projects are run and organised. These are often an important element in projects' communication strategies. Encouraging clients to participate in contract work (where this is available), visits (for example, to other projects, public gardens or parks), research studies and any media coverage of the project (with reference to appropriate consent procedures) also helps to strengthen links and understanding between all project members, as well as outside agencies and organisations.

Developing communication and social skills

A key role many STH projects play in promoting social inclusion, independence and understanding among clients is in helping them to develop their communication and IT skills. A large number of projects offer literacy and numeracy courses as well as IT programmes and training in other subjects such as book keeping and office skills.

There are many examples among projects of clients progressing in terms of their knowledge and IT skills, for example, to such an extent that they either leave to take up paid employment or they join the project team and work on promotion, advertising and communication strategies themselves.

However, not all projects are able to offer such training, and indeed a number of project organisers themselves do not have the skills to promote training in this area. An important aspect of project development is to ensure that project staff have the necessary experience and training to develop training programmes themselves.

While a significant outcome of STH is the promotion of social inclusion and interaction, developing clients' social skills and networks is not always a specific or pre-defined objective of many projects' intentions. For many clients, forming new friendships and associations is often an inevitable and natural outcome of project attendance, since gardening and horticultural activities mainly rely on the efforts and commitment of teamwork.

However, the way in which most projects are structured and organised means that they inevitably facilitate the formation of friendships and confederacy, whether or not this is a specific project objective. For example, most projects have structured breaks and meal times where clients, volunteers and staff can get together informally. Some projects organise day trips or visits to public gardens or horticultural events.

While most projects offer clients the opportunity to work on their own, if that is what they want, on the whole the type of work that clients and volunteers undertake more often involves people working alongside one another. Some clients also travel to and from projects together. While most clients do not extend the friendships they form at projects sufficiently to continue the associations outside project time, some clients do meet up in their own time for leisure or sports activities.

Increased access to new and more extensive social networks is a critical feature of the benefits of client attendance at STH projects. Most vulnerable clients do not, in their daily lives, have the opportunity to form new friendships or associations. Indeed, many vulnerable people are socially excluded because of the nature of their vulnerability (for example, if they have serious mental health problems, learning or other difficulties). STH projects can make an important contribution to clients' quality of life by enabling them to feel less marginalised or isolated.

Self-advocacy

STH projects enable clients to be heard by involving them in the management process and teaching them the necessary skills and knowledge in order to take part in that process. This helps to build self-confidence and independence that is useful in other areas of their lives such as obtaining appropriate help and support. Projects can assist this further by forming 'self-advocacy' groups, particularly for those with learning difficulties. There are a number of organisations and networks that specialise in helping with the formation of these groups.

One garden project that was visited by the researchers had recently started self-advocacy groups for all of their clients with learning difficulties. They were helped by a local organisation that ran training sessions and provided teaching materials for them. The group has learned to organise meetings, cast votes, set up a bank account and manage the funds (it makes around £500 a year from sale of arts and crafts at festivals). It will then decide what the money is to be spent on – members want day trips – they also want new furniture for their cabin and have been quite vocal in expressing their opinions. Self-advocacy groups build confidence for clients to speak up for themselves and to be taken seriously.

There are many local self-advocacy groups and there is an initiative in progress at present to form a national network of groups. Further details are available from Central England People First: www.peoplefirst.org.uk/

Networks and partnerships

Projects all face similar challenges – funding, client referrals, availability of resources, ideas for activities, recruitment of staff and volunteers and so on. There are many ways in which they can help each other, for example, by the exchange of ideas on fundraising activities or forming partnerships for them; loan of equipment and tools as many expensive tools and items of machinery are used infrequently so loaning them to other projects preserves valuable resources, and they can also be bought in partnership; expertise such as computing and IT skills can be shared; and joint activities can be carried out. Networks, therefore, both formal and informal, are an important part of project life. Around 1,000 projects are part of the national network supported by Thrive; they were included in the network by responding to a survey of projects and receive a regular newsletter and details of events and training. New projects can join by contacting the charity. Local networks can be formed to stage specific events, for example, projects in the West Midlands hold an annual flower show. Informal networks can be formed on an ad hoc basis to respond to specific events or circumstances such as new government initiatives or legislation. Partnerships and association with other organisations and forums can be particularly useful for raising awareness and sharing resources. These include allotment associations, horticultural societies, conservation groups, green partnerships, food initiatives, organic networks and many others. Many potential volunteers and clients may not be aware of the existence of the projects or even of the whole area of social and therapeutic horticulture.

Links with colleges and universities can also be fruitful, although few projects appear to have such connections. One project regularly held a stall at the local university's freshers fair to publicise their activities. Through that they were able to recruit volunteers who were able to attend not only during the vacations but also in term time – Wednesday afternoons are traditionally reserved for sports and voluntary activities by colleges and universities. The project workers also discovered to their surprise that there was a demand for organic produce by the students as fresh food was not available on the university campus that was located some way from the town centre and any shops. They are now considering a box scheme or market stall. Many universities and colleges also provide information about voluntary work as part of their Community Action initiatives or careers service, and establishing contact with those departments can also be very useful.

Building relationships with care agencies and professionals

It is important that projects have effective communication strategies in place to develop links with health and social care agencies. Initially, this might involve projects identifying a specific member of staff to liaise with practitioners in health and social care organisations and to help raise awareness about the benefits of STH for vulnerable groups.

Health and social care professionals often have heavy caseloads and little time to dedicate to work outside their own field of expertise. In which case, it is the responsibility of projects to help raise awareness by, for example, organising seminars or specific visiting times for health or social care practitioners to see for themselves how projects are structured. Projects could also ensure that their promotional material, newsletters and website details are targeted at specific practitioners responsible for making client or patient referrals (some projects produce dedicated promotional material about their work, such as videos or CDs, which are aimed at specific health professionals, for example, GPs).

Specific approaches such as inviting health practitioners, for example, psychiatrists and community mental health workers, to case meetings at projects or inviting health or social care professionals to join project management committees or trustee boards are just two examples of how STH projects can improve communications and relationships with health and social care agencies. In some cases, where appropriate, project workers are asked to attend case meetings at care homes and hospitals as they are often the people who know the client best.

It would also be useful for project staff to have some understanding and knowledge about government policy and legislation, for example the National Service Frameworks, which are strategies that set national standards and identify key issues for particular groups, for example, those with mental health needs or older people (see www.nhsia.nhs.uk/nsf); and the 1995 Disability Discrimination Act, as well as some insight into the state benefits system.

Summary

Engage in promotional work and advertising strategies in order to raise awareness about the project and its work.

Develop effective communication strategies between organisers, clients and volunteers/helpers.

Offer education, IT and training opportunities to clients where appropriate.

Enable clients to develop friendship networks during their time at the project.

Promote social inclusion by integrating clients in the project team and in local communities (think about holding open days, seed swaps, plant sales).

Consider participating in advocacy schemes.

Develop effective communication strategies between project staff and practitioners in health and social care agencies.

Ensure project staff have some understanding about policy and law.

Storage and use of personal information

Projects are likely to collect and store a variety of personal and sensitive data on their clients. This may include addresses and telephone numbers, medical histories, criminal records, and assessments of abilities. This has to be used and stored in accordance with the eight principles of the 1998 Data Protection Act, which covers not only computer records but any other form of data, including written notes. Compliance with the law is the responsibility of the 'data controller', that is, the person who controls access to the information. This will usually be the project organiser or manager. The eight principles of the Act are:

1. **Personal data shall be processed fairly and lawfully.** Clients should know why the information is being collected, how it will be used, to whom it will be passed and for how long it will be kept.
2. **Personal data shall be obtained for specific and lawful purposes and not processed in a manner incompatible with those purposes.** Information obtained for a specific purpose must not be used for other purposes.
3. **Personal data shall be adequate, relevant and not excessive in relation to the purpose for which it is held.** Unnecessary information should not be collected.
4. **Personal data shall be accurate and, where necessary, kept up to date.**

5. **Personal data shall be kept only for as long as necessary.** For example, do not keep files of people who have left the project unless you have a particular reason for doing so.

6. **Personal data shall be processed in accordance with the rights of data subjects under the Data Protection Act.** 'Data subjects' – clients and members of staff whose personal data is kept by the project – have a right to know what information is kept about them and have the right to take action to correct or destroy any information that is inaccurate.

7. **Appropriate technical and organisational measures shall be taken against unauthorised or unlawful processing of personal data and against accidental loss or destruction of data.** Information must be stored securely on computers using passwords or encryption. Other files must be locked. Information must not be passed to third parties unless permission is obtained from those to whom it relates, or it is passed as part of the legitimate activity of the project, or to protect the health or vital interests of individuals. Care must be taken when disposing of confidential data, for example, paper records should be shredded or burned and redundant computer disks should be wiped clean before disposal.

8. **Personal data shall not be transferred to a country or a territory outside the European Economic Area unless that country or territory ensures an adequate level of protection for the rights and freedoms of data subjects in relation to the processing of personal data.** There are exceptions to this principle, for example, if transfer of information is in the interest of the client.

(The wording in bold is the exact wording of the Act, other notes are explanatory.)

Further information regarding data protection is available from the Information Commissioner's Office: www.informationcommissioner.gov.uk/

Summary

Only collect and store information that you actually need.

Ensure all records are stored securely.

Clients and staff have a right of access to stored information.

Project policy statement

This guide has discussed a number of issues related to running a STH project and has made suggestions and recommendations. Some of these issues lend themselves to the preparation of policy documents to inform staff and clients alike of the procedures and practices adopted by the project and its aims and objectives. A set of policy documents can be collected together in the form of a project handbook that can be made available to staff, clients and referring agencies. These are not 'set in stone' but develop and change as the project grows and matures or as requirements or circumstances alter. A policy handbook can include the following:

- The project name and its identity.
- A statement of the aims and objectives of the project.
- The client group and policy on acceptance of clients.
- Staff requirements, job descriptions, recruitment and selection methods and criteria.
- Policy on recruitment and selection of volunteers, for example CRB checks.
- Policy on employment of ex-offenders.
- General human resources policies and procedures, including those on grievances and disciplinary matters.
- Assessment of clients – assessment method, period of assessment.
- Progression pathway within the project.
- General health and safety policy including risk assessment.
- Data storage policy – compliance with Data Protection Act.
- Induction procedures and checklists for new staff, volunteers and clients.

5 Conclusion

Conclusion

In this guide we have looked at social and therapeutic horticulture in respect of promoting social inclusion for vulnerable people (those with learning difficulties, mental health problems, physical disabilities and so on). This guide is not intended as a step-by-step manual on setting up a STH project as there are a number of guidance documents and reports already available on this subject (see Appendix B).

However, for anyone working in health and social care practice, in voluntary or statutory agencies and organisations, it will hopefully serve as a useful guide to using STH as a way of promoting social inclusion among a wide range of groups. STH offers a number of opportunities to help people with mental or physical health or other problems feel more confident and able to work with others as well as, for example, to think about and plan their own future employment, work or education opportunities.

The practice of STH can also help foster independence, security and friendships in natural settings, with few of the strict work-related pressures often associated with paid employment. Some of these and other benefits of STH are explored in *Health, well-being and social inclusion: Therapeutic horticulture in the UK* (Sempik et al, 2005), the companion volume to this practice guide.

While in many respects it may seem obvious that any project that is intended to help and support vulnerable groups in communities should observe and adhere to principles of effective management, coordination of services and support and health and safety issues, it has not always been clear in the past what these principles are or should be in respect of promoting social inclusion. Factors such as the nature and extent of STH activities, risk assessments, health and safety procedures, education and training are all important elements of STH project design and implementation.

While we have included guidance and protocols for a number of different aspects of project management and organisation in this guide, these should not be seen as obstacles to implementation of STH projects but should be viewed as informative and constructive approaches to effective STH service delivery.

Other factors, such as the opportunities projects provide for clients to develop their social skills, independence and increase their self-esteem are equally important in respect of providing effective and long-lasting STH services. These and other issues have been addressed in this guide and set out in such a way as to facilitate further understanding about the needs of vulnerable clients and how these can be met through attendance and activity at STH projects.

Appendices

Appendix A

Getting started: a checklist for anyone considering starting a new project

Some of the readers of this guide may be interested in starting their own project. Most projects are founded on the strength and enthusiasm of individuals and small groups who have worked long hours to achieve their success. However, hard work and commitment are not the only hallmarks of a successful project. The following checklist should help any prospective project organiser to determine whether there is a need for the project in the first place and will assist in the compilation of a feasibility report or business plan.

A need for the project
- Is there a need for your project?
- Do you know about other projects in your area?
- Have you visited them?
- Have you worked or volunteered for them?
- Is there an established network of local projects?

The client group
- Who will your clients be?
- How many clients will use the project?
- What are you going to deliver?
- What will the clients gain?
- Do you need transport for your clients?

The staff
- Realistically, how many staff and volunteers will you need?
- How will you recruit them?
- What skills should they have?
- Do you need to carry out any 'checks' on potential staff?
- Are contingency plans adequate, for, example, staff leaving?

Skills, training and contacts
- What skills do you have, for example: horticultural, counselling, nursing, teaching, working with vulnerable groups, management, financial, social?
- What training do you need?
- What local contacts do you have with prospective employers, sponsors, social services?

Assessment and progress
* How will clients be referred?
* How will you assess the benefits to your clients?
* Are they likely to find employment or enter education or training?
* Will they stay indefinitely?
* How will they progress at the project?
* Who will replace the first cohort of clients?

Financial management
* Where will your start-up funding come from?
* How will your running costs be met?

The project site
* Is your proposed site suitable?
* Will you have security of tenancy in the short, medium or long term?
* Is the site physically secure? Can it be made secure and how much will it cost?
* Are the facilities adequate, for example, water, access, parking?
* Is there space on the site for shelter, administration, food and drink preparation?
* Has a feasibility study been carried out?

The local community
* What impact will your project have on the local community?
* Have you consulted with local residents and others about the project?

Legislation and regulations
* Are you aware of relevant current legislation, for example, employment, health and safety?
* Are there any local restrictions? For example, do you need planning permission to erect sheds, polytunnels or greenhouses? Are you likely to get it?

The future
* How would you like the project to develop?
* How long will you stay with the project?
* How will you find a replacement?

Appendix B
A bibliography of textbooks and useful publications for STH projects

Title	Author(s)	Publishers	Date	ISBN number
Healing gardens: Therapeutic benefits and design recommendations	Clare Cooper Marcus and Marni Marcus Barnes	John Wiley & Sons Inc (Healthcare & Senior Living Design Series)	1999	04711192031
Green nature, human nature: The meaning of plants in our lives	Charles A. Lewis	University of Illinois Press	1996	252065107
The healing fields: Working with psychotherapy and nature to rebuild shattered lives	Sonja Linden and Jenny Grut	Francis Lincoln in association with the Medical Foundation for the Care of Torture Victims	2002	0711220271
Growth through nature: A preschool program for children with disabilities	Stephanie M. Molden, Nancy K. Chambers, Matthew J. Wichrowski, Gwenn Fried, Harvey Loomis, Vincent Chiu	Sagapress	1999	0898310423
Growing with gardening: A twelve-month guide for therapy, recreation and education	Bibby Moore	The University of North Carolina Press	1989	0807818305
Healing gardens	Romy Rawlings	Weidenfeld Nicolson Illustrated	1999	1841880337
Horticulture as therapy: Principles and practice	Sharon P. Simson and Martha C. Straus (eds)	The Food Products Press	1997	1560228598 (hardback) 1560227949 (paperback)
Gardening: An equipment guide	Fred Walden	The Disability Information Trust	1997	187377317X
Horticultural therapy and the older population	Suzanne E. Wells (ed)	The Haworth Press Inc	1997	0789000458
Accessible gardening: Tips and techniques for seniors and the disabled	Joann Woy	Stackpole Books	1997	0811726525

Occupational therapy books useful for the Diploma course in Therapeutic Horticulture

Title	Author(s)	Publishers	Date	ISBN number
Evidence-based practice for occupational therapists	M. Clare Taylor	Blackwell Science	2000	0632051779
Groupwork in occupational therapy	Linda Finlay	Nelson Thornes	1993	0748736360

Appendix C
Contact details of useful organisations

Organisation	Contact details
American Horticultural Therapy Association (AHTA)	909 York Street, Denver, CO 80206, USA Tel: (00 1) 303-370-8087; www.ahta.org
Black Environment Network	1st Floor, 60 High Street, Llanberis, Wales, LL55 4EU, UK Tel and Fax: +44 (0)1286 870715; www.ben-network.org.uk
British Association for Counselling and Psychotherapy	BACP House, 35-37 Albert Street, Rugby, Warwickshire CV21 2SG, UK Tel: +44 (0)870 443 5252; Fax: +44 (0)870 443 5161; www.bacp.co.uk
British Trust for Conservation Volunteers (BTCV)	Conservation Centre, 163 Balby Road, Doncaster, South Yorkshire DN4 0RH, UK Tel: +44 (0)1302 572 244; Fax: +44 (0)1302 310 167; www.btcv.org
College of Occupational Therapy	106-114 Borough High Street, Southwark, London SE1 1LB, UK Tel: +44 (0)20 7357 6480; www.cot.org.uk
Cultivations	Nant yr Helyg, Maentwrog, Blaenau Ffestiniog, Gwynedd LL41 4HF, UK Tel and Fax: +44 (0)1766 590480; www.cultivations.co.uk
Environmental Trainers Network	c/o BTCV, 47-50 Hockley Hill, Hockley, Birmingham B18 5AQ, UK Tel: +44 (0)121 507 8390; Fax: +44 (0)121 507 8391; E-mail: ETN@unite.net www.btcv.org/etn
Federation of City Farms and Community Gardens	The Green House, Hereford Street, Bedminster, Bristol BS3 4NA, UK Tel: +44 (0)117 923 1800; Fax: +44 (0)117 923 1900; www.farmgarden.org.uk
Health and Safety Executive, Publications	HSE Books, PO Box 1999, Sudbury, Suffolk CO10 2WA, UK Tel: +44 (0)1787 881165
Henry Doubleday Research Association (HDRA)	Ryton Organic Gardens, Coventry, Warwickshire CV8 3LG, UK Tel: +44 (0)24 7630 3517; Fax: +44 (0)24 7663 9229 E-mail: enquiry@hdra.org.uk www.hdra.org.uk
Horticulture for All (Federation to Promote Horticulture for Disabled People)	c/o Institute of Horticulture, 14/15 Belgrave Square, London SW1X 8PS, UK www.horticultureforall.clientpreview.net/about.asp
National Open College Network (NOCN)	9 St James Court, Friar Gate, Derby DE1 1BT, UK Tel: +44 (0)1332 268080; Fax: +44 (0)1332 268081; E-mail: nocn@nocn.org.uk www.nocn.org.uk
National Proficiency Tests Council	Avenue 'J', National Agricultural Centre, Stoneleigh, Warwickshire CV8 2LG, UK Tel: +44 (0)24 7685 7300; Fax: +44 (0)24 7669 6128 E-mail: information@nptc.org.uk www.nptc.org.uk
National Society of Allotment and Leisure Gardeners (NSALG)	O'Dell House, Hunters Road, Corby, Northants NN17 5JE, UK Tel: +44 (0)1536 266576; Fax: +44 (0)1536 264509 E-mail: natsoc@nsalg.demon.co.uk www.nsalg.org.uk
People Plant Council	Department of Horticulture, Virginia Polytechnic Institute and State University, Blacksburg VA, 24061-0327 USA www.hort.vt.edu/human/PPC.html
Royal Horticultural Society	80 Vincent Square, London SW1P 2PE, UK Tel: +44 (0)20 7834 4333; E-mail: info@rhs.org.uk www.rhs.org.uk
The Sensory Trust	Watering Lane Nursery, Pentewan, St Austell, Cornwall PL26 6BE, UK E-mail: enquiries@sensorytrust.org.uk www.sensorytrust.org.uk
Thrive	The Geoffrey Udall Centre, Beech Hill, Reading RG7 2AT, UK Tel: +44 (0)118 988 5688; Fax: +44 (0)118 988 5677 E-mail: info@thrive.org.uk www.thrive.org.uk
Women's Environmental Network	PO Box 30626, London E1 1TZ, 4 Pinchin Street London E1, UK Tel: +44 (0)20 7481 9004; Fax: +44 (0)20 7481 9144 E-mail: info@wen.org.uk www.wen.org.uk

Appendix D
Risk assessment

As gardening projects become more integrated into the system of health and social care provision there is an increasing demand from local authorities and social services, who refer clients, for formal risk assessment. Risk assessment is simply a logical way of asking questions about the activities and features on a project site and identifying *hazards* and *risks*. A hazard is the potential for an object or activity to cause harm or injury while risk is the likelihood that harm will be caused by that hazard. Many publications on risk assessment take a 'five-point view', for example, the following steps are taken from the Health and Safety Executive's booklet '5 steps to risk assessment' (available free from the HSE Books, PO Box 1999, Sudbury, Suffolk CO10 2WA, tel: +44 (0)1787 881165 or downloaded from the Internet; see www.hse.gov.uk/pubns/raindex.htm).

The 'five-point' view of risk assessment:

1. Look for the hazards.
2. Decide who might be harmed and how.
3. Evaluate the risks and decide whether the existing precautions are adequate or whether more should be done.
4. Record your findings.
5. Review your assessment and revise it if necessary.

Appendix E
CRB disclosure certificates

A 'Standard Disclosure' gives details of a person's convictions, including those classified as spent under the 1974 Rehabilitation of Offenders Act, and any warnings, cautions or reprimands that are held on the police national computer. An 'Enhanced Disclosure' includes any additional information held by local police forces in their records. The CRB check also establishes if the person's record is on any lists held by the Department of Health (DH) and the Department for Education and Skills (DfES) of people considered unsuitable to work with children or vulnerable people. Since July 2004 a new list is maintained by the DH as part of the Protection of Vulnerable Adults (POVA) scheme.

It is a legal requirement that those working with children and who are are checked against the lists held by the DfES and DH; and that those who work with vulnerable adults in care homes or provide domiciliary care (care in the homes of vulnerable adults) are checked against the POVA list. These checks can only be carried out by the CRB. Projects that are run by local authorities, the NHS or charities may have requirements for CRB checks as part of their operating policies. It may also be a condition of insurance cover. There is a cost for CRB disclosure certificates – £28 for a Standard Disclosure and £33 for an Enhanced Disclosure, but certificates are free to volunteers.

Application for disclosure is made by the employee or volunteer and countersigned by the employer (each receives a copy of the disclosure but the employer may be sent additional information considered relevant by the CRB). However, in order to make the application, the employer needs to be registered with the CRB. Registration costs £300 and the 'Registered Body' must comply with the code of practice drawn up by the CRB and the Scottish Criminal Records Office. This includes, for example, the requirement of a written policy for the employment of ex-offenders. It will be impractical for small organisations or projects to become Registered Bodies but if they wish to use disclosures they may do so by using a 'Registered Umbrella Body', which will provide access to the service on their behalf. Some charities and voluntary organisations act as Umbrella Bodies for CRB checks, as do some units within local authorities. There are also private companies that will apply for CRB checks on behalf of organisations and projects, but they charge a fee to their clients (around £12-£20 per person, usually with a reduced fee for unpaid volunteers).

Further information is available from:
The Criminal Records Bureau (www.crb.gov.uk and www.disclosure.gov.uk)

Details about the POVA list are provided on the DH website:
(www.dh.gov.uk [search for 'vulnerable adults']).

Printed and bound by CPI Group (UK) Ltd, Croydon, CR0 4YY

09/06/2025

14686546-0001